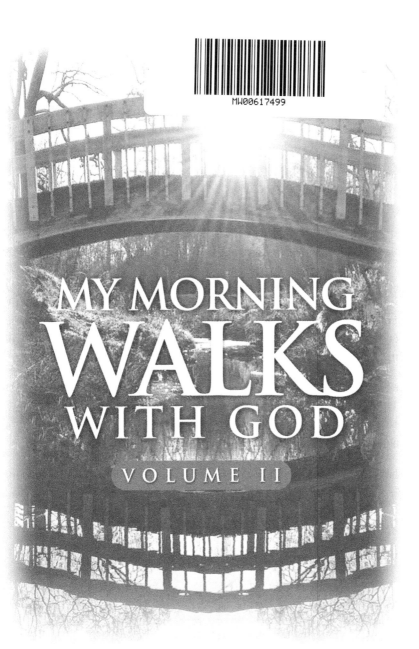

MY MORNING
WALKS
WITH GOD

VOLUME II

A Six-Month Journey Filled with
Reflections, Revelations and Recollections

GREG A. LANE

My Morning Walks with God

ISBN 978-0-9984882-1-9

Published by Inspired Design & Graphics

PREFACE

TAKE A WALK... WITH GOD

Then the man and his wife heard the sound of the LORD God as He was walking in the garden in the cool of the day, and they hid from the LORD God among the trees of the garden. - Genesis 3:8

Genesis 3:8 tells us that Adam and Eve heard the sound of God walking in the Garden in the cool of the day. From this scripture, I get the impression that God was in the habit of taking a walk with Adam and Eve in the Garden, perhaps as part of a daily routine. But, on the day that they sinned, they no longer wanted to walk in fellowship with Him as they had done in the past. Instead, they hid from Him. Their sin created a separation between them and the God they once walked with. God lost His walking partner.

Throughout the scriptures we find a recurring theme of God desiring to restore His broken relationship with man. Why did He want man restored? So He could once again walk with him, closely.

Think about Enoch. We know nothing of this man of God except for the fact that the scripture says, "Enoch walked with God" (Genesis 5:22, 24). Evidently, he enjoyed such a rich relationship with God as he walked with Him that God just took him on to Heaven without him having to undergo the pains of death. God reminds us in Micah 6:8 that He wants us to "Walk humbly with your God." And, in the New Testament we're reminded that we must "Walk by faith, not by sight" (2 Corinthians 5:7).

When Christ died for our sins, our broken relationship with God was restored. God got His walking partner back!

We all can enjoy a rich relationship with God... the kind that Adam and Eve once had... the kind that Enoch had. In this relationship, we walk through life knowing that the invisible God is right by our side. And, because we know He is walking with us, we talk to Him as we walk along and enjoy the inspiration and revelation He shares with us as we open our lives up to Him.

That's what this devotional is all about. The devotions in this book were all written immediately after I've returned home from my morning walks with God. Thus the name of the book. Almost every morning, over the last 10 years, I've started my day off by taking a morning walk. During my walk, I spend time talking to God, and listening to what He has to say to me. He often gives me insights and inspiration that are so rich that I feel the need to share them with others. That's why I've written this book.

I pray that as you read this devotional your daily walk with God will be strengthened.

I hope you enjoy the walk!

WHY MORNING?

My voice shalt thou hear in the morning, O LORD; in the morning will I direct my prayer unto Thee, and will look up. - Psalm 5:3

If you read carefully through the scriptures you will see an underlying theme of morning worship. David referred to "awakening the dawn" in the book of Psalms (see Psalm 57:8 and 108:2). He also referenced morning as a time when he offered up his prayers for God's help and provision (Psalm 88:13, Psalm 119:147). It appears that there is something special about the morning time as it applies to communion with God.

In the gospels we read about Jesus rising early in the morning, many times while it was still dark, so He could go to a solitary place to pray and receive God's instruction for the day (Mark 1:35, Luke 4:42). Yes, morning seems to be an important time of the day for those who are in relationship with God.

Why is the morning so special? Because it's the FIRST part of our day. God wants our FIRST. As a matter of fact, the FIRST is so important to Him that Jesus said, "Seek ye FIRST the kingdom of God." FIRST is not just a priority level... it is a time of the day. Morning is our FIRST thoughts, FIRST words, and FIRST actions of the day. The way we start off in the FIRST part of the day will greatly influence how the rest of our day goes.

So, don't say, "I'm not a morning person." That's not a good confession over your life. That's like saying, "I'm not good at starting but I'm good at finishing." Starting and finishing go hand-in-hand. If you want to finish well, you've got to start well. Sure, you can read this devotional at night before you go to bed if you want to, but ultimately you'd be missing the whole point of why this book was written.

Start your day off right! Take a moment to walk with God.

LIGHT AS A FEATHER
January 1 | July 1

I had been experiencing an extremely difficult week. It felt like a ton of bricks was weighing down on me from the stresses of my work and from some disturbing national news that was burdening my spirit. Plus, I was dealing with the added grief of an unexpected death in my church family. So, I went on my prayer walk early in the morning, hoping to find some relief and peace. As I was discussing my feelings and emotions with the Lord and contemplating the many pressing deadlines that were looming overhead, something interesting captured my attention. About 20 feet above me and directly in front of me on the path I was walking, I saw something falling from the sky. It wasn't falling quickly. It was practically floating. At first I thought it was one of those helicopter seeds slowly falling from a nearby tree, but this was much larger, yet lighter.

As I walked forward I reached out and grabbed the object that glided down to me "from Heaven." It was perfectly timed to fall into my hand as I stayed in pace on my morning walk. It was a gray bird feather, either from a mocking bird or a dove. Yes… it was perfectly timed. As I saw how gently that feather floated to earth it was as if God was speaking to me about the weight I was carrying. The words of Jesus came up within me, "Come unto Me, all who are weary and HEAVY-laden and I will give you rest… My yoke is easy and my burden is LIGHT."

MY PRAYER FOR TODAY:
"Father, forgive me for carrying weights I was not meant to carry. You told me to cast my cares upon You, but so often I forget Your words and try to carry them myself. This world is trying to weigh me down and to steal my joy and peace. I can't give in to it. I chose to lighten my load by casting all my cares on You… for You care for me. In Jesus' Name I pray. Amen."

Matthew 11:30 (KJV)
For my yoke is easy and my burden is light.

Isaiah 61:3 (KJV)
To appoint unto them that mourn in Zion, to give unto them beauty for ashes, the oil of joy for mourning, the garment of praise for the spirit of heaviness.

LITTLE IRRITATIONS
January 2 | July 2

I took a meal with me to a nearby park to enjoy a little time outdoors during my lunch break. I found a picnic table that was in a nice, peaceful, shady spot. Everything was just right for a pleasurable moment of dining solitude. Then it happened. A fly began to buzz around me. It tried to light on my food. I swatted and waved my hands frantically to deter the little pest. He flew away and, for a moment, it seemed I had succeeded. He came back, though, a minute later with a few of his friends. They were buzzing all around me, and I was swatting, slapping, waving and becoming very irritated! My moment of solitude was completely disrupted by the pesky flies. I had to cut my lunch short. The moment was ruined because of the annoying pests.

That's when I was reminded that one of the names for Satan is "Beelzebub" which means "Lord of the Flies." Doesn't that make perfect sense? Flies are small irritating pests. So, when you put it all together, Satan is the "Lord of Little Irritations." Sure, he'd like to bring catastrophes and calamities of monumental proportions to you and me, but he's most effective at bringing small irritations our way that disrupt our peace and steal our joy. That's what he is "LORD" over… that's what he is best at… little irritations.

I know some people are going through major struggles and turmoil in their lives and I would never discount that for a second. But, the majority of us are dealing with small irritations that are almost insignificant, yet we let them steal away our peace and joy. Just remember, when you're going through those minor irritating circumstances that "The Lord of the Flies" is at work. He can't win, though, if we refuse to let the little irritations get to us.

Hold on to your peace and joy even in the midst of the little irritations you're experiencing and you'll have victory over Beelzebub… "The Lord of the Little Irritations."

Song of Solomon 2:15 (NAS)
Catch the foxes for us, The LITTLE foxes that are ruining the vineyards, While our vineyards are in blossom.

THE POWER IN A SEED
January 3 | July 3

It was around mid-June when my wife and I noticed a sprout of some kind of plant growing in our backyard flower garden. By the shape of the leaves we figured it to be a pumpkin or cantaloupe vine. We didn't intentionally plant it there. It came from a random seed that was accidentally dropped in that spot. All the elements worked together to nurture that seed. There's very little soil in that particular spot since it is covered with landscape fabric and river pebbles, yet there were just enough nutrients for the seed to take root and grow. At first we thought of uprooting it, but I wanted to see if even in its less-than-ideal situation it would be able to produce fruit on its vine.

By September, that little seed that barely had enough soil to take root, had developed into a full-grown plant. And, we discovered that it was neither cantaloupe nor pumpkin… it was a butternut squash vine.

I know I probably sound like a nature nerd when I say this but "SEEDS ARE COOL!" Just a couple of months earlier that plant didn't even exist… the leaves didn't exist… the flowers on the vine didn't exist… the squash didn't exist. All of it came out of a tiny little seed that pressed through all the adversity around it and grew, in spite of it all.

Seeds have incredible power wrapped up inside a tiny shell. I think that's why Jesus was always telling the disciples, "The kingdom of God is like a seed." There are at least three parables where Jesus used seeds to describe the kingdom of God. A person who has the kingdom of God planted inside them can do incredible things. They can grow in spite of adversity. And, not only can they GROW… they can also PRODUCE FRUIT. A person who has the kingdom of God inside of them doesn't need perfect conditions to be able to grow and thrive. Their power comes from the kingdom, and the kingdom has life within itself, just like a seed.

Child of God, the kingdom of God is growing inside of you. The kingdom of God can make you fruitful, no matter how harsh or difficult your surroundings might be. Don't lose heart. The fruit is on its way. The kingdom of God is powerful, and it's in you… so YOU'RE POWERFUL.

Matthew 13:31 (NIV) "The kingdom of heaven is like a mustard seed…."

AM I WRONG?
January 4 | July 4

Wouldn't you hate to find out that you were wrong about something that you thought your whole life you were right about? I'm not talking about being wrong about insignificant things, either. I'm talking about really important things that are crucial and eternal. Every once in a while, just like this morning, I feel the need to pray, "Lord, if I'm wrong in any area where I think I'm right, show it to me so I can make adjustments." If I'm wrong in people's eyes, that's one thing. But, if I'm wrong in God's eyes that's another story.

I don't want to be "right" so I can win an argument or debate. I don't want to be "right" so I can feel good about myself and look down my nose at those who are wrong. I want to be right because that's what God is… He's RIGHTeous… and I want to be like Him… and I want to be on His side. When you're right with God, it gives you a special confidence. You're not worried if other people say you're wrong. You don't even necessarily feel compelled to prove you're right. Being right with God is its own reward.

In the book of Judges, you will see a phrase repeated over and over again… "in those days THERE WAS NO KING in Israel; everyone did what was RIGHT in his own eyes." That's where the world is today. Man does not allow God to be his king, so he makes up his own rules with no regard to the truth of God's Word. It's a very dangerous way to live. As a Christian, I must not succumb to the value system of this world. I can't make my own decisions about what is right and what is wrong. I need a basis, a standard, to follow. So, I test my beliefs and values against those found in God's Word, The Bible, and make adjustments accordingly.

TODAY'S CHALLENGE:
Take an inventory of your life. Get really honest with yourself and with God and ask Him to show you where you're not RIGHT. And when you realize you've been wrong about something, repeat this prayer of David when he discovered that he was WRONG… "Create in me a clean heart, O God, and renew a RIGHT spirit within me." Psalm 51:10

Psalm 19:12 (KJV)
Who can understand his errors? Cleanse thou me from secret faults.

WHEN DID THOMAS "GET SAVED"?

January 5 | July 5

Romans 10:9 tells us what a person needs to do to be saved: "If you confess with your mouth Jesus as Lord and believe in your heart that God raised him from the dead, you will be saved." So, you've got to believe in the resurrection of Jesus Christ... it's important to your salvation. Now, think back to after Jesus rose from the dead. He had appeared to all the disciples except for one... Thomas. (Otherwise known as "Doubting Thomas.") Thomas was not with the other disciples the first time Jesus appeared to them. So, when the disciples told Thomas that Jesus had risen from the dead, Thomas replied, "Unless I see in His hands the imprint of the nails.... I WILL NOT BELIEVE." Now, think back to what Romans 10:9 says we must believe in order to be saved... we must believe that God raised Jesus from the dead. So, in essence, the other disciples were "saved" because they believed in the resurrection, but Thomas was not, because he didn't believe. What an interesting "theological predicament!"

Jesus appeared again to the disciples, eight days after the resurrection (John 20). This time Thomas was in the room with the other disciples. Jesus made a special effort (if you will) to ensure that Thomas got his opportunity to "see the imprint of the nails in His hands." When Thomas saw Jesus, he believed in the resurrection and fell at Jesus feet saying, "My LORD and my God" (John 20:28). So, Thomas BELIEVED in the resurrection, PLUS he confessed that Jesus was LORD".... the two things Romans 10 tells us must take place in order for a person to be saved. It was then that Thomas "got saved!"

In the middle of the most important event in the history of mankind, the resurrection of Jesus Christ, we read the story about someone who doubted the resurrection... who refused to believe it... and it was one of Jesus' closest friends! Jesus was merciful in allowing Thomas the opportunity to see the nail imprints in his hands. He even told Thomas to stick his hand into Jesus' side where the spear had pierced him. But, he did offer a small rebuke to Thomas. He said, "Because you have SEEN you have BELIEVED. Blessed are those who have not seen and still believe." Friends, that's us! I've not seen His resurrected body, but I believe... and Jesus says I'm blessed for believing. Not only that, I'M SAVED! I believe in the resurrection of Jesus Christ, and just like Thomas I call Him, "My LORD and my God!"

THE IMPORTANCE OF WAITING
January 6 | July 6

The stop light had just turned green and I waited for the line of cars ahead of me to start moving in the North-bound lane of Sparkman Street... but not a single one of the eight cars ahead of me moved an inch. Ten seconds passed, then 15 seconds... then 20. Still no movement in the traffic. The first car in the line was wanting to turn left, but there was no left turn traffic light. Cars in the South-bound lane were driving by, almost mockingly, as our North-bound lane remained at a standstill. Boy, was I frustrated! Finally, the first car got an opening in the traffic and made their left turn. What sweet relief! Our line finally began to move. It was short-lived, though. The light immediately turned red. Seven cars remained ahead of me. We would have to WAIT another minute or so for our light to turn green again.

As I sat there and fumed I was convicted by my lack of patience. "Why does WAITING make me so angry?" I wondered within myself. The Spirit of God within me answered my question instantly... "It's because of pride." As I thought more about it, it made perfect sense. My pride was saying, "I'm too important to sit here and wait on somebody else. I've got things to do and people to see. I shouldn't have to wait." Yes, that was the source of my anger... my stinking pride.

Now, here's a little bit of history for you. In the olden days of the monarchy, queens had a special female servant that attended to all of their needs. That person was called a "Lady in WAITING." Their only purpose in life was to serve the queen. They themselves had no identity of their own to speak of. Their identity was wrapped up in WAITING on the queen. Any need that arose, the Lady in Waiting would handle it for the royal highness. There was no place for pride or self-importance.

Likewise, the Christian has been called to serve the Lord... to attend to the needs of their King. In doing so, their own pride and self-importance must be subdued. "Waiting on the Lord" does not mean that we're sitting idly by, twiddling our thumbs, waiting for Him to do something. Instead, it is understood that we WAIT on Him, just like the Lady in Waiting waited on the queen, attending to her every need. Waiting on others, and on God, can be a very humbling thing. There's no room for pride. The more we WAIT the less pride can remain in us. But, remember. God promises in the book of Isaiah, *"They that WAIT upon the Lord will renew their strength."* I'd much rather have God's strength than my pride. How about you?

I'M A LIFE PRESERVER
January 7 | July 7

"You can't be a life preserver if you have an anchor tied around your neck."
I heard those words rise up inside my heart on my walk one morning.
Now, I don't know if I just made that up, or if I had heard it somewhere
before, or if it came straight from the throne of God. All I know for sure
was that it was a very convicting thought!

I'm here, on this earth, for a reason. Part of my purpose is to help other
people. If I'm always weighed down with my own problems, worries and
cares I'll be of little use to others who need my help. There's a good reason
why the scripture says, "Cast all your cares on Him" (1 Peter 5:7) and, "Lay
aside every weight" (Hebrews 12:1). Weights and cares pull us down... and
you can't be a life preserver if you have an anchor tied around your neck.

WORRY

Worry is a care
That was never released in prayer
So it continues to stay right there,

Whispering in your ear,
"God is nowhere near."
It's a devilish fear!

It becomes a doubt,
The whisper becomes a shout,
"God's not able to work this out!"

Before you know it, this thief
Has robbed you of belief
And filled your heart with grief,

Because you listened to a whisper
From the lips of the truth-twister
And you weren't a resistor.

Resist the devil and he will flee from you - James 4:7

POSITIVE OR NEGATIVE?
January 8 | July 8

I was in a discussion with some people about a particular song and singing group, and I chimed in with, "I don't really like that singing group." Just a couple of minutes later I thought to myself, "Why did I feel the need to express my negative opinion? Why couldn't I have just kept my mouth shut as opposed to voicing negative comments?"

Do you ever just stop and listen to the negatives that come out of your mouth? I've become increasingly more convicted of this the older I get. Many make the excuse, "I'm older now, so I can say whatever I want to say." The truth is, the older we get the more caution we should be using when we speak. We're old enough and experienced enough to know the repercussions of the words we speak and how influential our words can be, either positively or negatively.

So here are two questions I must ask myself today…
1. Am I best known for negatives or for positives?
2. Do people know more about who I am because of the things I support or the things I'm against?

Think about God for a moment. What is He best known for? For His love, of course. It actually almost confuses us when we read passages in the scriptures that say "God hates." Yet it is true that there are things that God hates (Proverbs 6:16-19). But, the thing He is best known for is His love. John 3:16 doesn't say, "God so HATED sin that He gave His only son." No! It says, "God so LOVED the world that He gave His only son." His love for man is what motivated His actions… not His hatred for sin.

So here's a challenge for today… BE POSITIVE. Be known as a positive person. Be known for the things you support not the things you're against. If you feel the need to voice your opinion, have something good to say. Remember the old adage: "If you can't find something good to say, say nothing at all."

Proverbs 13:3 (NLT)
Those who control their tongue will have a long life; opening your mouth can ruin everything.

HOW GOD SEES THINGS
January 9 | July 9

Every Wednesday night after our Discipleship group is over I always ask the boys in my group if they want to take home the 2 liter drink bottle that we have left over. One night, however, there wasn't any drink left... just an empty bottle sat on the table. Still, just for fun, I said, "Who wants to take the drink home with them tonight?" The boys said, "There's not any drink left, Mr. Greg, you can throw it away." I replied, "Okay, that's what I'll do." With that, I drop kicked the bottle like a football and kicked it up into the air and then caught it. When the boys saw what I did with the bottle they immediately said, "Cool! No, don't throw it away... We want it!" For the next 5 minutes they tossed the bottle around like a football and played catch with it. One moment it was nothing more than garbage to them... the next moment it was an object of value, fun-filled, not worthy of the garbage can.

I like it when people see the potential and value in something that they didn't see before. Maybe I like it so much because I know that's the way God sees people and things. He doesn't see things the way people do. People see a scrawny little shepherd boy... God sees a king. People see a man with no children... God sees a Father of many nations. People see 5 loaves of bread and 2 fish... God sees a feast for 5,000 people. People see a Roman torture device... God sees the salvation of the whole world!

MONDAYS

No athlete ever won a race by cursing the starting gate. The way you start will determine the way you finish. As a matter of fact, adjustments that you make while in the starting gate can make all the difference between winning or losing at the finish line. Having said that, why do people curse their Mondays? It's the starting gate of our work week. The way we start will determine how the rest of the race will go, and what will await us at the finish line. Don't curse your Monday by saying, "Good Lord. It's Monday." Instead, try saying, "Good! Lord, it's Monday!

1 Corinthians 9:24 (KJV)
Know ye not that they which run in a race run all, but one receiveth the prize? So run, that ye may obtain.

THE LORD GOES AHEAD OF ME
January 10 | July 10

On my walk one morning this scripture verse popped into my heart: "The LORD is the one who goes ahead of you" (Deuteronomy 31:8). I spoke those words over and over again to myself as I walked along. Then I took a moment to reflect on all that it means.

The Lord is making a way for me. He's going ahead of me and preparing my pathway, removing hindrances and roadblocks. He's giving me level roads to walk on. As I sat and reflected on those thoughts, it was then that I remembered two strange dreams that I had earlier that morning before I awoke. Strange because they were both dreams about road construction. In both dreams there was a road crew working on the road I was driving on, and I was told to wait for their signal before moving forward. I was incredibly irritated that I was having to wait in both of these dreams. In one of the dreams I actually took a detour so I wouldn't have to wait. Can you see the significance of these dreams as they relate to the scripture verse that popped up in my heart?

If God is going ahead of me and preparing the road for me, it is important that I let Him finish His work before proceeding. I've got to stay on the road that He's put me on. If it's under construction, I will just have to wait. If I'm going to the place He's preparing for me, then it's going to be awesome. I can't take a detour to avoid waiting on the construction. A detour will not take me to the place He's wanting me to go. I must be patient. If I have to wait before taking the next leg of my journey then so be it. As long as I know that He is ahead of me, making my path straight and smooth, there's no cause for alarm… or impatience.

MY PRAYER FOR TODAY:
"Lord, help me to trust what You're doing in my life. I don't want to get ahead of You. I will be patient as You prepare the way ahead of me. I won't take any of the detours that this world offers me. Lord, help me be patient."

Deuteronomy 31:8 (NAS)
The LORD is the one who goes ahead of you; He will be with you. He will not fail you or forsake you. Do not fear or be dismayed.

TOUGH, AND TENDER
January 11 | July 11

I woke up one morning and discovered four long scratches on my arm. I had no idea where they came from. I went over in my mind all of the things I did the previous day and couldn't remember the moment in time when I got scratched. I was just a little bit puzzled by it.

When I was a kid, I could tell you *when* and *where* every scratch, cut and bruise came from. When you're a kid, whenever your flesh gets wounded you remember. But, when you get older, wounds don't impact you the way they used to. For example, as I write this devotion today, I see a blood clot under my right thumbnail. It's been there now for over 2 months and I still can't remember when, where or how I mashed my thumb.

So, what's my point? We all get wounded in life, physically, emotionally and even spiritually. If you're able to keep up with the time and place every wound ever happened to you, it's possible that you haven't grown up yet... it's a sign of immaturity. In Bible school I had a teacher who instructed the class with these words, "Have the hide of a rhino." What he was saying was, "Don't let things get to you.... Be thick-skinned." I know it's easier said than done, but it's definitely something worth pursuing.

Be tough on the outside, and tender on the inside... what a challenge that is in today's world!

1 Corinthians 13:4-5 (NIV) "Love... keeps no record of wrongs."

GOD HOLDS ALL THINGS TOGETHER

Colossians 1:17 (NIV)
He is before all things, and in Him all things hold together.

Do you realize that God is holding everything together? In the universe, in the Earth, and even in the smallest molecules that exist... God is holding EVERYTHING together. If He can hold the universe together, surely He can manage your life. People who say, "My life is falling apart," need to rediscover the power of God in their lives... for He is the one who holds all things together!

LORD, CHANGE MY ATTITUDE?

January 12 | July 12

I was on my walk one morning when a prayer left my lips that caused me to do some thinking. I prayed, "Lord, change my attitude where it's wrong." I began to wonder if that is truly a prayer that God would answer. Does He really CHANGE people's attitudes?

I know He changes our hearts, and our lives and He will even change our eternal destiny, but is He in the business of changing our attitudes? I thought back to when I was a kid, still living under my father's roof. When my attitude was wrong, I'd get sent to my room with the admonishment, "Don't come out until you've changed your attitude!" My mom and dad tried to CORRECT my attitude, but they left the CHANGE up to me. I had to be able to see how damaging my attitude was, the trouble that it could get me in, and the way it affected my life... those things would help me bring the change to my attitude that was needed.

THEY CORRECTED... I CHANGED.

I believe that is the way God deals with the wrong attitudes in His children as well. If He CHANGED our attitudes without us being involved in the process we'd never comprehend the effect our attitudes have in our lives. Yes, I believe God will CORRECT our attitudes by saying, "You need to adjust your attitude," but He leaves the CHANGE up to us. There is a certain amount of energy and self-control that we will need to exert in overcoming our wrong attitudes. It's called "becoming mature."

So, I changed my prayer. I prayed, "Lord, correct my wrong attitudes. Show me where my attitude is wrong so I can make the adjustments that are needed... so I can be a better representative of Your kingdom. In Jesus' name I pray, Amen."

Revelation 3:19 (NLT)
I correct and discipline everyone I love. So be diligent and turn from your indifference.

Jeremiah 10:24 (KJV)
O LORD, correct me, but with judgment; not in thine anger, lest thou bring me to nothing.

HEARING IS BELIEVING
January 13 | July 13

I took my son on a trip out west for his high school graduation in 2012. While on our flight, I didn't see the pilot of the plane one single time. I heard a voice come over the intercom. The voice said he was the pilot, but for all I know it could have been a recording. Somehow that metal tube with wings carried me and my son halfway across the country. I believe there was a pilot who flew us there, but I have no firm evidence of the pilot's existence. The only thing I know for sure was that I heard his voice.

I hear people say, "I'd believe in God if I could just see Him." I wonder if they feel the same way about airplane pilots? On my flight out west I didn't see one person demand evidence of the pilot's existence. I didn't see one person ask for the pilot's credentials or past flying experience. Nor did anyone ask if he made good grades in flight school. We just blindly believed that the pilot was skilled and able to do what needed to be done. One hundred human beings put their life in his hands! No, I didn't see that pilot one single time... but I heard him, and that was sufficient for me to believe in him.

We all have faith in the unseen, whether we know it or not. We don't have to SEE God to believe in Him. The only thing we need is to hear His voice (the Bible... God's Words). He will get us safely to our destination if we will simply trust His voice as He leads us.

Doesn't the Bible tell us plainly that "Faith comes by HEARING"? If that is the case, why are we always demanding to SEE something from God? Those who say they need to SEE God before they'll believe in Him should not be hypocrites... they should request to see the pilot of the next plane they fly in before they allow the plane to leave the ground!

MY PRAYER FOR TODAY:
"Father, thank You for the Word of God. Thank You for the direction You give me from Your Word. Thank You that my faith is strengthened when I hear Your voice speaking through Your Word. I don't have to SEE YOU to believe... HEARING YOU is enough for me!"

Romans 10:17 (KJV)
So then faith cometh by hearing, and hearing by the word of God.

A SOUND MIND
January 14 | July 14

2 Timothy 1:7 says, "For God hath not given us the spirit of fear, but of power, and of love, and of a SOUND MIND." I've often confessed this scripture verse over me and my loved ones in respect to our mental health, emphasizing the words "sound mind."

I looked up this scripture one morning in several different versions of the Bible and saw something I hadn't seen before. I noticed that some versions of the Bible replace "sound mind" with "discipline" and/or "self-control." That's because "sound mind" comes from the Greek word *sophronismos*, which carries the connotation of "self-control." How interesting is that!

According to God's Word, soundness of mind is directly connected to self-control. If I'm understanding the connection correctly, it would appear that those who have a difficult time with self-control in their lives might eventually struggle with mental deficiencies. When you think about it, it makes good sense.

Self-control isn't just about pushing away from the supper table before you over-eat. Self-control also means keeping a tight grip on the things you think about internally. We can't continually think on negative, worrisome, fearful thoughts all the time and expect that to result in good mental health. No. The person who wants to have good mental health should use self-control and intentionally make themselves think on things that are good, wholesome and pleasant. That's why Paul tells us in the book of Philippians, "Finally, brothers and sisters, whatever is true, whatever is noble, whatever is right, whatever is pure, whatever is lovely, whatever is admirable--if anything is excellent or praiseworthy—THINK ABOUT such things" (Philippians 4:8).

Do you want to have good mental health? Of course you do! It starts with self-control. Exert some self-control over the things you THINK today. Don't let your mind dwell on negative, critical, worrisome thoughts. Take control!

Proverbs 25:28 (NLT)
A person without self-control is like a city with broken-down walls.

YOUR TRUE VALUE
January 15 | July 15

I was trying to help my son sell his truck, so I agreed to keep it over at my house where people could come test drive it while he was at work. We had quite a few "lookers" who came by to test drive it, but no one seemed interested in buying it at the asking price. I was confident, though, that the truck was worth the price we were asking. I even told my son that I would buy the truck for myself if no one else would buy it at that price.

One day, two guys came to give the truck a test drive. They looked like they just came off the set of Swamp People. One of the guys was big and gruff, with a scraggly beard. He did all the talking. After their test drive he asked about the price on the truck. I told him the asking price and he just snickered and said, "Good luck getting that for this truck!" He began to rattle off a list of things that was wrong with it. I'm pretty sure he was waiting for me to say, "Well what would YOU give for it" but I held my ground. I was aware of all the problems, but I also knew that they could be fixed somewhat easily. So, with great confidence I said, "I'm sure I'll get the price we're asking."

Now, up to that point I was certain of the value I had placed on the truck. But that man's words kept on reverberating in my ears, "Good luck getting that for this truck!" I began to doubt the true value of the truck.

I'm telling you, that's just like the devil! God tells you how much value we have in His eyes, and the devil comes along and says, "Yeah, right. They've got too many problems… too many issues that need to be worked on. They'll never be worth that much!" We often doubt our value because of the devil's accusations. But, God has already proven our worth and value. He paid an awesome price to gain us as His children… he paid the price of His Son's life. You see, it doesn't matter what the devil says you're worth. What matters is what God says you're worth… He's the One who purchased you!

Oh… now the rest of the story. Later on that same week a man came by and bought my son's truck… at the price we were asking. He knew the true value of the truck, just like I did.

1 Corinthians 6:20 (NAS)
For you have been bought with a price: therefore glorify God in your body.

I CAN
January 16 | July 16

In your ear, the devil wants to plant
A two-word phrase… the words "I can't."
If your permission you will grant
He'll reduce you down to a tiny ant.

But there's a two-word phrase of which I'm a fan,
And it's spoken by the Christian man
Who understands God's power and plan.
The two-word phrase? The words "I CAN."

When I meet challenge face-to-face
I won't resist it, I'll embrace
And put my trust in my God's grace
For He said I CAN win this race.

When obstacles mount I won't think twice
I'll quickly heed the Bible's advice
It tells me God's strength will suffice
And I CAN do all things through Christ.

The words "I can't" we all should ban
They tend to make us all "less than"
And they don't fit into God's plan.
The phrase that does? The words "I CAN!"

Philippians 4:13 (NLT)
For I can do all things through Christ, who gives me strength!

PRAY....

How should you pray? Pray...
• Like your prayer will make a DIFFERENCE… it will.
• Like your prayer is the KEY that will unlock the blessing… it is.
• Like your life DEPENDS on it… it does.

James 5:16 (KJV)
The effectual fervent prayer of a righteous man availeth much.

BALANCED
January 17 | July 17

BALANCED: having different parts or elements properly or effectively arranged, proportioned, regulated, considered, etc.

I like that definition. "Properly or EFFECTIVELY ARRANGED." Whenever you see balance you know that some thought and planning went into it... it was "arranged" that way. Balance doesn't happen "by chance." No. Where there is balance there is "a balancer." My checkbook is balanced only because I took time to EFFECTIVELY ARRANGE my deposits and my withdrawals. If I eat a balanced meal it is because I took time to EFFECTIVELY ARRANGE groupings of food on my dinner plate that are wholesome and healthy choices. When our lives are out-of-balance we know it's because we haven't taken the time to EFFECTIVELY ARRANGE our schedule, eating habits, relationships, etc.

Think about addictions. An addiction happens when one thing in a person's life has gotten out-of-balance and becomes overemphasized at the expense of all the other parts of their life. An addict is a person who has gotten out-of-balance... their lives are no longer EFFECTIVELY ARRANGED.

God is an EFFECTIVE ARRANGER... He is The Ultimate Balancer. He puts just the right amount of things, people, work, and time into our lives to bring complete balance. We're the ones who mess things up and get too much of one thing or another in our lives that create imbalance within ourselves.

Can a person have true balance in their lives? Yes, but only if they allow The Ultimate Balancer to EFFECTIVELY ARRANGE their lives.

MY PRAYER FOR TODAY:
"Lord, bring balance to my life. Show me how to EFFECTIVELY ARRANGE all that you've given me so that I can maintain the balance You created me to have."

Phillipians 1:6 (NLT)
And I am certain that God, who began the good work within you, will continue his work until it is finally finished on the day when Christ Jesus returns.

BELIEVERS
January 18 | July 18

You could go to church your whole life and that wouldn't make you a believer. Going to church doesn't make you a believer… believing does.

You could pray every day of your life and that wouldn't make you a believer. Praying doesn't make you a believer… believing does.

You could donate all your time and money to charitable causes and that wouldn't make you a believer. Giving yourself sacrificially to ministry doesn't make you a believer… believing does.

There's a reason why a believer is called a believer. They BELIEVE.

And, it's not just that they believe in God, because the book of James reminds us that demons also believe in God and tremble (James 2:19). They believe something very specific… they believe in JESUS. They believe that He is the Son of God. They believe there is power and authority in His name. They believe He is their only hope for salvation and restored relationship with God. They believe He conquered death, hell and the grave at His resurrection. That's what makes them BELIEVERS.

Before Jesus left this Earth and ascended to Heaven, He said something very important to His disciples. He said, "These signs shall follow those who BELIEVE in my name…"(Mark 16:17). Signs and miracles don't follow churchgoers, pray-ers, or givers… they follow BELIEVERS.

MY PRAYER FOR TODAY:
"Lord, I want to do Your work in this Earth. I know the only way that will happen is through believing in Your name. Through the name of Jesus I can do mighty things for You. Strengthen my belief in the name of Jesus!"

Mark 9:23 (KJV)
Jesus said unto him, If thou canst believe, all things are possible to him that believeth.

John 1:12 (KJV)
But as many as received him, to them gave he power to become the sons of God, even to them that believe on his name.

THE RAINBOW AROUND GOD'S THRONE
January 19 | July 19

Isn't it amazing all the colors we find in nature? On my morning walks I often spend time thanking God for the gift of color I see all around me. How bland and boring nature would be without all the vibrant colors God has provided for us to enjoy.

Did you know that God loves color so much that He has a rainbow that surrounds His throne? Revelation 4:3 says, "And the one who sat there had the appearance of jasper and ruby. A rainbow that shone like an emerald encircled the throne." There's no doubt that God loves color since He encircles his throne with it!

Now get this... there are also people who surround His throne who have come from every tribe, nation and tongue, who continually praise and worship His name forever. Yes, people of ALL COLORS surround God's throne, in the same way that the rainbow of all colors surrounds His throne.

So, why would anyone believe one race is superior to another? Why would anyone believe that people of different skin color should not be associated with, or mingled with? God made people of all colors. He did it on purpose. Are there any colors in the rainbow that are superior or inferior?

Imagine taking one of the colors out of the rainbow. How strange would it be to see a rainbow with no yellow in it? Were the color yellow removed from the rainbow, the colors would go from red, to orange, to green. Yellow brings a smooth transition between orange and green. As a matter of fact, orange and green are both made from yellow. Orange is a combination of red and yellow, and green is a combination of blue and yellow. Remove yellow from the rainbow and you essentially would have to remove orange and green as well.

All colors are important. God loves a variety of colors.... we should too!

Revelation 5:9 (NIV)
And they sang a new song, saying: "You are worthy to take the scroll and to open its seals, because you were slain, and with your blood you purchased for God persons from every tribe and language and people and nation."

CONNECTED
January 20 | July 20

There's a word that's been rolling around in my mind and heart for a couple of years now as I've been on my morning prayer walk. The word is CONNECTED. I find myself saying and praying that word often. "Lord, help me CONNECT to You and to Your kingdom today. Help me be CONNECTED to the most important things in life and to DIS-CONNECT from the things that are distractions and unimportant." I remember one morning that word was particularly emphasized during my prayer time and I wondered if I was supposed to share it with others.

When my walk for the day was over, I went and sat down at my computer. The screen saver was in full operation so I clicked on the mouse to deactivate it. I had forgotten that I had plugged my wireless keyboard into my computer to recharge its low battery. As soon as I unplugged the USB cord from the keyboard this word popped up on my screen…. "CONNECTED." My computer was letting me know that the keyboard was fully charged and in sync. But, more importantly, God was letting me know that the word "CONNECTED" needed to be shared with others. So, I wrote a social media post that morning called "CONNECTED."

Today, I'll ask you the same question I asked others on that particular morning: "Are you CONNECTED to God?" No, I didn't ask if you go to church. I didn't ask if you're "saved." I didn't ask if you know you're going to Heaven. All of those things are important, but that's not what I'm asking. I'm asking if you have a viable, living, interactive connection with God? Are you connected to His heart and mind? Are you connected to what He is doing in the Earth, or are you doing your own thing, hoping He approves? Listen, you can live in the same house with another person and have no connection with them… that's not much of a relationship, but you could fool yourself into saying you're connected with them. Do you engage with God? Do you talk to Him? Do you listen for His voice? Do you follow where He says to go? There are definite ways to measure if you're connected. So, I ask you today… are you CONNECTED?

2 Corinthians 13:5 (NIV)
Examine yourselves to see whether you are in the faith; test yourselves. Do you not realize that Christ Jesus is in you--unless, of course, you fail the test?

BOUNDARIES
January 21 | July 21

I took my dog, Archie, with me on my morning walk and discovered that the city had removed the fence between the cemetery where I walk and the road next to it. They were getting ready to put in a brand new fence to replace the old one. Well, the old fence had always served as Archie's boundary line from the time he was a puppy. I'd release him from his leash and the fence contained him within the boundaries of the cemetery, keeping him out of the busy street beside the cemetery. So, on that particular morning, before I released Archie from his leash, I talked to him for a moment.

"Archie, there's no fence today to keep you out of the street. You've got to keep your own boundaries today." Now, I know Archie didn't understand a single word I said, but I felt compelled to repeat my command to him. "You've got to keep your own boundaries." I guess you could say that the Lord was speaking to me through my own words spoken to my dog, because a light came on inside me when I said those words.

How do you know when you've achieved a measure of maturity in your life? When you can keep your own boundaries. When you know where the boundaries are and you refuse to test them. Some people look at boundaries as if they're prison walls, keeping us from experiencing all the fun and freedom that life offers. But, in reality, our boundaries are walls of protection. Let's face it. We've got an enemy that wants to destroy us. Jesus said, "The thief comes to steal, kill and destroy." As long as we stay within the boundary lines of God's protection we remain safe.

When we were younger we needed physical reminders of where those boundaries are, just like Archie needed when he was a puppy. But now that Archie has matured, he knows where he can and cannot go to remain safe.

So here's a thought for today. Are you mature? Do you know where your boundaries are? Or, are you still testing the boundaries God has set up in your life for your own protection?

Job 1:10 (GOD'S WORD® Translation)
"Haven't you put a protective fence around him, his home, and everything he has?" (Words of Satan spoken to God concerning Job)

GET CHARGED UP!
January 22 | July 22

Every night before I go to bed I plug my phone into the charger to replenish the battery. There have been a couple of times I've forgotten to do so, so in the morning when I get ready to start my day and notice I've not charged my phone yet, I have to plug it in and wait. It's got to sit there and charge for a while before it's ready for another day.

We have all of these wonderful illustrations around us that remind us of our daily need to connect with God… just like that phone charger. Isaiah 40:31 reminds us, "They that WAIT upon the Lord will renew their STRENGTH." Do you need STRENGTH? We are no different than that cell phone which DAILY needs to be replenished with strength from an energy source. We have an energy source in our lives, too…. and it's not supposed to be a little bottle of 5 Hour Energy drink, either.

Our strength comes from the Lord. But, when are we allowing time for the energizing process in our lives? We charge our phones DAILY because the battery gets depleted after one day. Yet, people will go a full week (some longer than that) without re-energizing themselves in the Lord.

So, how does a person get charged? Just like Isaiah 40:31 says, you've got to WAIT… you've got to get still and get connected to God, the source of our strength. It takes a little time. It takes focus. You've got to get "plugged in" to the power source.

Do a little mental/spiritual exercise today. Draw on a piece of paper what you think your battery supply level is... what is your STRENGTH level? Do you feel like you're fully charged? 50%? Almost depleted? Has the red light come on saying, "Low Battery Mode"? Be honest. Is it time to get charged up? It doesn't happen automatically. If I don't "on purpose" plug my phone up to the charger before I go to bed at night, my battery will die in the early morning hours the next day. By the way, just going to church once a week doesn't charge you up for one whole week. Just try charging your phone one time a week and see how far that gets you.

Psalm 27:14 (International Standard Version)
Wait on the LORD. Be courageous, and he will strengthen your heart.
Wait on the LORD!

THE KINDNESS OF HIS HEART
January 23 | July 23

I pulled into the Hardee's Drive-thru line one morning about the same time another guy did. There have been times when I've actually had other people race to get ahead of me in line in similar situations. But, this guy was different. When he saw me coming, even though he had gotten there a couple of seconds before me, he didn't demand his place in line. He waved me in to the line ahead of him. It was such a rare moment and such a kind gesture that I felt compelled to do something kind in return.

After I placed my order and paid for my food at the window, I then paid the tab of the man in the car behind me. Kindness should be rewarded with kindness, don't you think? Anyway, as I drove off I began to think about the exchange that just took place. You see, I have no idea who that man was. He could have been a Christian, or an unbeliever. He and I might have completely different opinions on government and politics. He could have been rich, or possibly, poor... happily married, or going through a nasty divorce. I have no idea what his life is like. But, what I do know about the man was that he showed a kindness in a world where few take the time to do so.

Kindness begets kindness and blessing begets blessing. The opposite is also true. Rudeness begets rudeness and cursing begets cursing. The Bible is clear. Whatever a person sows, that's what they're going to reap.

Surely it was the Lord Himself who spoke to my heart this morning and said, "Pay for his meal." And, I don't doubt that it was the Lord Himself who spoke to that man's heart saying, "Let that guy pull in ahead of you." Don't you think so? Doesn't that sound like something God would do? I believe when we're compelled to do an act of kindness for someone else we're just responding to God's voice in our heart.

I hear people say, "The devil made me do such and such," or "The devil has been tempting me all day long" as if the devil talks to us more than God does. Nonsense! God speaks to our hearts often and tells us things to do, and we do what we're told, thinking that we are doing it out of the kindness of OUR heart, when in reality, we did it from the kindness of HIS heart.

Galatians 5:22 (NAS)
But the fruit of the Spirit is love, joy, peace, patience, KINDNESS....

TWO PENNIES
January 24 | July 24

I know God loves me and is looking out for me, but sometimes I forget how much He works even in the smallest details of my life. For instance, one morning, while on my morning walk, I happened to look down and saw a penny laying in a crack of the sidewalk. I picked it up and stuck it in my pocket, not giving it much thought. As I walked along further, about 300 yards away, I found another penny laying on the ground, right there in front of me. So, I picked that penny up and thought to myself, "This is too much of a 'coincidence' to be just a coincidence. I wondered what the significance might be of finding two pennies laying on the ground. I continued my walk with those two pennies tucked away in my pocket.

Later on that day, I decided to go to a drive-thru for lunch. After I completed my order the cashier told me the price would be twelve dollars and some change. Oh, yeah... the amount of change was TWO CENTS. I completely forgot the two pennies I had stuck in my pocket that morning, so I scrounged around to find some change in my truck's console. As soon as I handed the cashier my money it was then that it hit me... I had TWO CENTS in my pocket from this morning! It was too late, though. My opportunity to see God at work in the smallest details of my life was not fully realized that day until after it was too late. BUT, at least I have this story to tell.

I want to get sharper and keener every day. I want to be more aware of God's work in my life. I know He's doing so much more than I give Him credit for, and that particular day I found out just how blessed I am for being in a relationship with "The God of the Smallest Details."

MY PRAYER FOR TODAY:
"Lord, help me be more aware of Your work in every area of my life. I know you make even the smallest details work together for my good. I anticipate today that even my smallest needs are met by Your provision."

Luke 12:6-7 (NIV)
Are not five sparrows sold for two pennies? Yet not one of them is forgotten by God. Indeed, the very hairs of your head are all numbered. Don't be afraid; you are worth more than many sparrows.

THE NEWEST VERSION OF THE WILL
January 25 | July 25

I watched "from the outside" as I saw a family torn apart after their loved one passed away. The Will of the deceased had been updated (unbeknownst to much of the family) several months before their death, and the entire estate was bequeathed to just one member of the family. All other members of the family were completely removed from the Will. I looked on helplessly as I saw firsthand what greed can do to people. But, I also learned a very important piece of information about inheritances and wills.

A Last Will and Testament gives all of the details about how a deceased person's belongings and inheritance are to be divided. If there is an older version of the Will and a newer version, the newest version of the Will is the one that takes precedence. For instance, if your great uncle Fred left you nothing in the first draft of his Will, but later amended the Will/Testament and left you with one million dollars, the FIRST Will is made obsolete by the LAST Will (Thanks Uncle Fred!!). The OLD is made obsolete by the NEW. Most Wills actually include verbiage which states something to the effect of: "If there is conflict between this amendment and the Agreement or any earlier amendment, the terms of this amendment will prevail."

The Bible is divided into two TESTAMENTS (WILLS). There is an OLD version and a NEW version. I like reading about things that happened in the OLD, but I remind myself that the NEW is where I find the verbiage detailing what my inheritance is. Any place where there is a conflict between the two TESTAMENTS I know that I find the final authority in the NEW... It is more legally binding. The contract and verbiage in the NEW overrides anything found in the OLD.

So here's some advice for today. Read and learn all you can from the Old Testament, but always remember that the New Testament is where your inheritance is found. When Jesus died, an updated version of God's Will was made available to us. It is called the NEW TESTAMENT, or in legal terms, it is THE LAST WILL AND TESTAMENT OF JESUS CHRIST.

Luke 22:20
This cup is the NEW TESTAMENT in my blood, which is shed for you.

THE SOUL IN THE MIDDLE
January 26 | July26

My wife and I went on a walk together one morning and we brought our dog, Archie, along with us. My wife was walking faster than I was, so we were separated by about 200 yards. At one point I looked up and saw Archie, halfway in between the two of us, looking forward towards my wife, then backward towards me. He was perplexed. He wanted to be with both of us, but it was impossible to do, so he was trying to make a decision about which of us to go to. In a couple of seconds he made up his mind. He ran forward towards my wife. Makes sense to me. After all, she's the one that feeds him every day.

Here's my thought for today. We humans are a 3-part being. We are spirit, soul and body. Our spirit and our body are seldom in complete alignment. The body (flesh) wants to do its own thing and the spirit desires to do what pleases God. That puts our soul (our will... our decision maker) in the middle. The soul wants the body and spirit to be in complete unity and agreement, but because they seldom are, the soul makes a decision as to which of the two it will join forces with. Who will the soul unite with... spirit or body? The answer is simple... the one that feeds it the most.

CAN YOU SEE WHAT I'M SAYING?

I was teaching a Bible Study and we were talking about *spiritual vision*, and how it differs from our *natural vision*. I was trying to convey the idea that there's more to see than what we see with our natural eyes. Ephesians 1:18 talks about the EYES of our heart. As I shared this, one person asked a question about what I was saying. He ended his question with, "Do you see what I'm saying?" I replied, "Yes, I SEE what you're saying." I said it again, "I SEE what you're saying." (I emphasized the word "SEE"). Could my physical eyes SEE words coming out of his mouth? No. As I emphasized the word "SEE" to him, it was like a light turned on for him. He understood even better than before that there are things we can SEE without using our natural eyes. Do you SEE what I'm saying?

Ephesians 1:18-19 (Berean Study Bible)
I ask that the eyes of your heart may be enlightened, so that you may know the hope of His calling, the riches of His glorious inheritance in the saints, and the surpassing greatness of His power to us who believe.

MISUNDERSTOOD
January 27 | July 27

My first and only "F" I ever received on a report card was in Algebra 2 during the first 6 weeks grading period of 10th grade. I didn't get an F because I was dumb, or lazy, or apathetic. It was because I thought I understood the formulas and principles of Algebra 2 correctly, but I was wrong. I'll say it this way: "I thought I understood, but in reality, I MISUNDERSTOOD." I was taking tests thinking "Man, I aced that one," only to get my test papers back with a big red "F" written at the top! Luckily for me, during the second 6 weeks grading period my teacher showed me what I was doing wrong and I corrected it. I raised that "F" to a "B" for my final semester average.

There's a really good reason why Proverbs 3:5 says, "Trust in the Lord with all your heart and lean not on your OWN UNDERSTANDING." Your OWN UNDERSTANDING could actually be a MISUNDERSTANDING… just like I misunderstood the formulas and principles of Algebra 2. I thought I understood, but I didn't. Had my teacher not corrected my wrong thinking in Algebra 2, I would have flunked the entire semester.

There are tests that we all face in life. We face those tests with the understanding we've acquired throughout our lifetime. But what if we've been given wrong information, or, what if we were given the right information but we misunderstood it, or misinterpreted it? Many people flunk the tests of life because they thought they UNDERSTOOD what the answer to their problems was, but they actually MISUNDERSTOOD.

Have you ever thought you understood a principle or a concept only to later find out that you misunderstood? It's embarrassing and humbling to admit it. What's really embarrassing is when you thought you understood the meaning of life only to later discover that you misunderstood. There are some people who don't discover the meaning of life until they're on their deathbed. Others thought they knew the meaning and later found out they were wrong when they stood before God's Throne. That's too late to be finding out! Don't lean on your own understanding… TRUST IN THE LORD.

Psalm 111:10 (NIV)
The fear of the LORD is the beginning of wisdom; all who follow his precepts have good understanding. To him belongs eternal praise.

MY MASTER
January 28 | July 28

I took my dog, Archie, with me on my walk one morning. As we passed by the dog park on the way, Archie was tugging at the leash, pulling in the direction of the dog park. I knew he wasn't going to be happy until we spent some time there first. So, we went to the park and he sniffed around, and we played fetch for a few minutes. Dog and Master spent time together. When it was time to go, I put him on the leash, looked down at him and said, "Now it's time for ME to spend time with MY MASTER." So, we walked on toward the cemetery where I take my morning prayer walk.

As I was walking along, this thought came to me. Isn't it interesting how God can redeem words like "master" and "slave." Think about it. Over thousands of years the words "slave" and "master" have had a very negative connotation. Yet, when Jesus walked this earth, people would often call Him "Master." He didn't rebuke anyone for using that word in reference to Himself. Not only that, He told many parables about slaves and masters, and used them as illustrations to show how the kingdom of God worked. His teaching was so replete with allusions to slavery that many today would find His message disturbing and offensive.

Paul spoke often of the freedom and liberty we have through Christ, yet he many times called himself a "bond-servant of Jesus Christ." Now, I'm in no way saying that human slavery is right or good, but isn't it interesting that God can take something that's seemingly unredeemable, such as slavery, and show us a truth about His kingdom through it? Would we fully understand what it means to call Jesus "MASTER" if not for the word "SLAVE?"

I am honored to be called His slave and His servant. I am honored to call Him MY MASTER. There is no shame in it, at all. Do you ever call Him Master? Or is it no longer politically correct to do so? Think about it.

Matthew 25:23 (NAS)
"His master said to him, 'Well done, good and faithful slave. You were faithful with a few things, I will put you in charge of many things; enter into the joy of your master.'"

GOD USES SURRENDERED MOUTHS
January 29 | July 29

Wouldn't it be great if God could use your mouth to bless someone else? I think He does it a whole lot more than we give Him credit. On one of my morning walks, I passed by another early-morning walker. We stopped and engaged in conversation for several minutes. Before we parted ways, I reached out and shook his hand and said, "Have a good day… Be blessed." Now, I had it in my mind to say, "Have a good day," but the "Be blessed" just kind of spilled out without me giving it any thought, so it took my by surprise. As I walked on, it was like the Lord said to my spirit, "See what I did there? I used your mouth to bless someone else."

Maybe that man didn't have anyone in his life that was speaking encouragement to him. Maybe he was going through a difficult time and God was wanting to reach out to him, but He couldn't find anyone who He could use as His mouthpiece. It was just two simple words, "Be blessed." But maybe those two words coming straight to him from God's heart gave Him the encouragement he needed to carry on in life. I don't know. All I know for sure is that those words came from my mouth, but not from my head or my own thinking… I know God used my mouth to speak through me to that man.

Yes, there have been times when I've purposely said, "Be blessed" to others, and I know it had an impact coming from me just because it was a positive, encouraging word. But I believe there are times, sometimes when we're not even aware, when God speaks directly through us to others, because we're willing vessels that He can use… because we've surrendered our lives to Him… and most importantly, because we've surrendered our mouths to Him.

MY PRAYER FOR TODAY:
"Lord use me as your mouthpiece today. I don't just want You to speak TO me… I want You to speak THROUGH me. I surrender my mouth to You today so You can use it to reach out and help those in need of comfort, encouragement and exhortation. In Jesus' name I pray. Amen."

Proverbs 18:21 (KJV)
Death and life are in the power of the tongue.

KNOWLEDGE IS RELATIONSHIP
January 30 | July 30

"...but from the tree of the KNOWLEDGE of good and evil you shall not eat, for in the day that you eat from it you will surely die." - Genesis 2:17

The word KNOWLEDGE in Genesis 2:17 is a derivative of the Hebrew word YADA, the same word (KNEW) that's found in Genesis 4:1, "Adam KNEW Eve his wife, and she conceived...." YADA means "to have intimate relations with." So, in the Garden of Eden, Adam and Eve were tempted by Satan to surrender their KNOWLEDGE of God (intimate relations with) so they could have a KNOWLEDGE of Good and Evil.

In our modern society we've completely misunderstood the meaning of KNOWLEDGE. Knowledge, in its truest meaning, is all about having a relationship with someone or something. We've confused "KNOWING" with "KNOWING ABOUT." Let me put it this way. What would impress you more: If I said, "I KNOW ABOUT the president," or if I said, "I KNOW the president"? To know about someone is fine, but nothing can replace knowing them personally... to be in relationship with that person.

So, here we are in the most KNOWLEDGE-FILLED time in history. People have KNOWLEDGE of all kinds of things through the use of modern technology (Internet, Google, 24-hour news, etc.). The problem is that we've developed a RELATIONSHIP with things–with science, with data and statistics, and with technological devices–instead of developing intimate relationships with people, and most importantly, with God.

I recently read that depression is up 33% higher than it was 5 years ago. So, here we are, with all of this KNOWLEDGE available to us, yet we're more unhappy now than we've ever been. Why? Because KNOWLEDGE is about intimate relationship, and when you have an intimate relationship with things, ideas, theories, statistics, data, and the like, none of those things can be "intimate" with you... they can't love you back. It's a one-way relationship, with no reciprocation. How depressing it can be when you're in a relationship where you're never acknowledged by the one you love!

What is the solution? It is found in going back to the beginning, before man substituted KNOWING GOD with KNOWING GOOD AND EVIL. To KNOW God is to have a relationship with Him. If you only KNOW ABOUT Him, you're missing the whole point of KNOWLEDGE.

PRAY FOR SOMEONE ELSE'S CHILD
January 31 | July 31

The following testimony took place right around the time of The National Day of Prayer in 2018. I pray it will be an encouragement to you as you pray for your loved ones.

My daughter had been looking for a full-time job in the Nashville area for almost 6 months without any luck. Of course, my wife and I had been praying for her during those months, believing for the right doors to open, but it seemed like our prayers were going unanswered.

Well, right around the seventh month of looking for a job, my daughter got called in for interviews with two different companies, so my wife and I "ramped up" our prayer efforts. I was praying diligently for her every morning, that her interviews would go well. A week later she got called back for a second interview, so I decided to spend some focused prayer time during my morning prayer walk on this particular interview. Oddly enough, though, just as I was about to start praying for her, I felt like God said to my heart, "Don't pray for her… pray for someone else's child now."

Doesn't that sound just like something God would do… to have you take your eyes off your own need and focus on someone else's need… to show Him that you trust Him… to show Him that you believe all the prayers you've already prayed have accomplished the work they were sent to do. So, I did as I felt instructed in my heart to do. I prayed for the children of several friends of mine that morning… and the next morning… and the next… and the next. My own daughter's name and needs didn't cross my lips in prayer for 3 or 4 days.

A week later we got a call from our daughter with the news, "I got the job! The one that I wanted!" Hallelujah! I danced a little jig in my living room when I heard the news! God is good!

Got a pressing need in your life? Don't be surprised if God calls you to take your focus off of it by praying for someone else.

Job 42:10 (NLT)
When Job prayed for his friends, the LORD restored his fortunes.

THE POWER IN A NAME
February 1 | August 1

I was talking to a young man who had recently gone through a very diffi-cult season in his life. He said that during that season of time, every time he would randomly open his Bible it fell open to the book of Ezekiel. He thought that was unusual, so he was looking for passages from that book that would bring him comfort and strength. When he said this, my heart was stirred within me. I said, "What does Ezekiel mean?" He answered, "Well, he was an Old Testament prophet that God spoke to." I replied, "No, that's WHO Ezekiel was, but I want to know what the name Ezekiel means." So, he looked up the meaning on his phone as I stood there. I didn't know what it meant, but I felt like the meaning was significant for him. He found the answer and said, "Ezekiel means 'God Strengthens.'" I'm telling you, a chill went down my spine when he said those words. Here's what I believe: I believe God didn't just want to say something to this young man in the chapters and verses of that book… I think God wanted to tell him something through the name EZEKIEL. God was tell-ing that young man, "God strengthens" every time he opened his Bible.

The meanings of people's names are all but lost to us today. In Bible days, a person's name had meaning, and people knew what the meaning was. Abraham, for instance, means "Father of many," Matthew means "gift of God," Seth means "appointed one," and Isaac means "laughter." Imagine that. When Isaac would walk up to a group of people they'd say, "Here comes laughter!"

Names are important. Not only are they important, they also carry power. There is one particular name that is so powerful that the Bible says when God speaks it "every knee will bow and every tongue will confess that He is Lord." That name is JESUS! Jesus isn't just a person's name, though. Jesus means, "Jehovah saves." When you speak the name of Jesus in prayer or praise, you're saying something very powerful… "Jehovah Saves."

Now if you're concerned that your own name has no meaning, remem-ber, God is known for changing people's names to something more fit-ting and meaningful. After all, He changed Jacob (meaning "supplant-er") to Israel (meaning "God Prevails"). In the book of Revelation, God promises this to the person who is an overcomer: "To the one who is victorious, I will give… him a white stone inscribed with a NEW NAME, known only to the one who receives it" (Revelation 2:17).

BORROWED TIME
February 2 | August 2

I remember hearing a pastor tell of his father's motto when borrowing things from other people… "Always return the borrowed object in better condition than it was given to you. If you borrow a car and the tank is half full, fill the tank before you return it to the owner. If you borrow a tool and it is dirty when you received it, clean it up before you return it." What an awesome way to ensure that people will always be more than glad to let you borrow from them.

There's an old saying that goes like this: "We live on borrowed time." Who did we borrow it from? God! Now, I don't believe for a second that He gives us any less than His best, so we can't return it to Him in better condition than the way it was received. But, that doesn't mean we shouldn't do our best to use it as wisely as possible.

So here's a question to contemplate today: Based on your current use of time, do you think God is inclined to let you borrow even more from Him?

Psalm 31:15 (KJV) - My times are in thy hand.

GUARD YOUR JOY

The Bible tells us that Satan is a thief. Thieves don't waste time trying to steal worthless stuff. So, why does the devil want to steal your joy? Because it's one of the most valuable things you possess. Why is it so valuable? Because it's the source of your strength! Remember what Nehemiah 8:10 says? "The JOY of the Lord is your STRENGTH."

Guard your joy carefully… like you would any other valuable thing that you possess. When you feel it slipping away you can be sure that the devil is trying to steal it from you. When your joy is stolen, your strength is gone. When your strength is gone, you're not able to fight against the enemy. STAY STRONG… PROTECT YOUR JOY!

Colossians 1:11 (NLT)
We also pray that you will be strengthened with all his glorious power, so you will have all the endurance and patience you need. May you be filled with joy,

CONFLICT
February 3 | August 3

In English class we learned that every story needs to have three elements in it to be considered a "good story:" 1) Conflict, 2) Climax, and 3) Resolution. A story without some kind of conflict that has to be overcome doesn't make for a very interesting story. As a matter of fact, a story without any conflict involved is usually downright boring... let's be honest about it.

Think about the great stories of the Bible. Wouldn't the story of Daniel be kind of boring without him being thrown into the lion's den? If Shadrach, Meshach and Abednego had bowed to the idol as the king had commanded, we wouldn't have the story of the fiery furnace. And, what if David had heard the threats and boasting of Goliath and turned around to go back home? Not much of a story there. The thing we like about these stories is that each person overcame their difficulties with God's help and grace.

If God had decided to continue the writing of the Bible to this day, would my life story be included in it? And, if it was included, would it be a story that would inspire people, or would they skip that chapter because of the boring content? As much as I hate to admit it, a little bit of conflict, trials and struggles adds interest to a person's life story.

So, I don't wish hardship on anyone today, but if you do face struggles and challenges, remember that God is watching and writing your life story. The way you handle the struggles will either bring you fame or shame. Overcome the conflict so your story can be one that others will tell for years to come... it's called "A Testimony."

Hebrews 11:32- 34 (NIV)
And what more shall I say? I do not have time to tell about Gideon, Barak, Samson and Jephthah, about David and Samuel and the prophets, who through faith conquered kingdoms, administered justice, and gained what was promised; who shut the mouths of lions, quenched the fury of the flames, and escaped the edge of the sword; whose weakness was turned to strength; and who became powerful in battle and routed foreign armies.

HIDDEN IDENTITY
February 4 | August 4

Our dog, Archie (a Boykin Spaniel), had us all fooled for the first 5 months of his life. In his first 5 months we never once heard him bark. Our previous dog, Lily (a German Schnauzer), was a barking machine! So, we thought we had a non-barking dog on our hands. Well, one day I took Archie to a pond. He had never seen a large body of water prior to that moment. Evidently Boykin Spaniels have a swimming instinct that has been bred into them, because when Archie (our non-barking dog) saw the water, something remarkable happened… he started barking at the water like he was talking to a new-found friend. It was as miraculous to me as the mute man who started talking after Jesus healed his speech impediment. Yes, that water stirred a hidden instinct in Archie, and he's been barking ever since. Just think, for 5 months he hadn't barked once, but that moment in time forever changed Archie.

Isn't it funny how one single event or moment in time can change who you are? There are things that you were born to do, to be, and to say, and when the right moment comes along it pulls all of that "destiny" out of you.

Jesus went to John the Baptist to be baptized in the Jordan River. When He came up out of the water, the Holy Spirit lighted upon him in the form of a dove and God's voice from Heaven said, "This is my beloved Son, in whom I am well-pleased." That moment in time is where His earthly ministry began… when He was 30 years old. Imagine that! Jesus had lived the life of an average, ordinary person for 30 years. There was preaching, teaching, healing and deliverance inside of Him, but none of it had yet been revealed. That moment in time is what catapulted Him into His destiny.

I suggest to you today that there are important life events that, as of yet, have not occurred in your life. The moment they do occur, things that were once hidden about your true identity and destiny will be unleashed. Some people think, "If it hasn't happened by now, it's probably not going to happen for me," but that's just not true. Jesus was 30 when He was baptized… Moses was 80 when he saw the burning bush… Sarah was 90 when she had the child (Isaac) that was promised by God. Hold on to the hope that says, "All that I am and all that I will be has not been fully revealed yet. God is working in me… when the time is right, the hidden things will be revealed."

UNFOLLOW
February 5 | August 5

UNFOLLOW... now that's a word that's not been around very long. The word didn't exist at the turn of the 21st century. Yet, today we use this word as a part of our regular vocabulary. "I UNFOLLOWED them on social media"... "I can't believe they UNFOLLOWED me!" It almost sounds ridiculous, doesn't it! It sounds almost as ridiculous as "I UN-LAUGHED at the joke he told. Sure, I thought it was funny at first, but after I thought about it I decided to take my laugh back."

Well, I was thinking about what "unfollow" means (to stop following somebody, particularly on social media) and the only other word that I can think of that means the same thing is disassociate (dissociate). So, even though the word unfollow is a new word, its meaning has existed for centuries.

Did you know that Jesus had some disciples (followers) that UNFOL-LOWED Him? They disassociated themselves from Him. Read John 6:66 (that's a scary number, isn't it?) and you'll discover that after Jesus said some hard things about discipleship, MANY of his disciples no longer followed him. Not just a couple... that scripture passage says MANY!

I feel certain that I've had people UNFOLLOW me over the years. And, to be truthful, I've chosen to UNFOLLOW a few people myself... people who I thought were someone different than they turned out to be. But how in the world could anyone UNFOLLOW Jesus? Yet, the Bible tells us it happened, and it still happens even today. There are people who once swore they'd live for Him all their lives who now don't even mention His name except as a byword.

I've been a FOLLOWER of Jesus for over 40 years now, and I've seen dozens of people who once served Him turn their backs on Him. I remember seeing one such person at a funeral I went to. I asked them, "Are you still serving the Lord?" Their answer shocked me: "No, I stopped doing that a few years ago." Even though I was shocked by their response, it didn't sway me in the slightest. You see, I'm a FOLLOWER of Jesus... and I've removed the UNFOLLOW button. How about you?

"I have decided to follow Jesus... no turning back, no turning back."

GOD ASKS QUESTIONS
February 6 | August 6

In the first two recorded conversations in the Bible between God and man, (found in Genesis 3 and 4) God asks a whopping eight questions. Four were asked of Adam and Eve, and four were asked of Cain. For a moment, let's not think about the content of the questions or the answers that were given. Instead, let's just think about the fact that the first recorded conversations of God in the Bible were jam-packed with questions. I think there's something here we should understand about God.

When God speaks to you and me, much of the time He is asking us questions. Think about it. When you've done wrong, inside your spirit you hear a voice say, "Why did you do that?" or "What were you thinking?" When you see a fellow human being in need you often hear a voice inside your spirit that says, "Are you going to help them?" or "What are you going to do?" When you go back to Genesis you find that God asked similar questions of Adam, Eve and Cain.

God may very well speak to you today. If He does, there's a really good chance the conversation will start with a question. Don't assume that the voice you're hearing inside of you is your own questioning voice. Genesis 3 and 4 makes it clear… God comes to us asking us questions.

Now, below is a list of the questions that God asked Adam, Eve and Cain. I'm positive I've heard at least a couple of these spoken to me over the past years... especially "What is this you have done?" and "Why are you angry?"

Genesis 3:9 - "Where are you?"
Genesis 3:11 - "Who told you that you were naked?"
Genesis 3:11 - "Have you eaten from the tree that I commanded you not to eat from?"
Genesis 3:13 - "What is this you have done?"
Genesis 4:6 - "Why are you ANGRY?" (God is asking this question A LOT these days!)
Genesis 4:6 - "Why is your face downcast?"
Genesis 4:7 - "If you do what is right, will you not be accepted?"
Genesis 4:9 - "Where is your brother?"

MISTAKEN IDENTITY
February 7 | August 7

When my kids were much younger, we had a cat named Michael. Now, Michael was the personification of the adage "Cats have nine lives." Michael had been a sickly cat most of his life. On top of the frequent ailments and illnesses he suffered through, he also had a few run-ins with a pack of neighborhood dogs. We were certain that his life span would be cut short, but he just kept on living!

Well, early one morning, my wife and I were walking down our street when we saw a dead cat in the middle of the road. As we got closer to inspect, we thought it was Michael. He had been run over by a car. All the markings on the cat were identical to Michael, so we picked the cat up and put his body in a bag to bury him. Our kids weren't awake yet when we got home. I was going to bury the cat while the kids slept so they wouldn't know of Michael's demise. Unfortunately, my daughter, Erica, woke up and saw what was going on, so we broke the news to her. She started sobbing. We took the lifeless body to a piece of property we owned down from our house, and I dug a hole as Erica stood there weeping. As I placed the body in the grave, I held Erica in my arms and spoke a few words to honor the dead cat. We stood there and wept and got all of the mourning out of our system.

When we got back home, my son, Ethan, was awake. We told him what happened to Michael. Then, I sat down at my computer and began my work for the day. About 30 minutes later, Ethan called out to me, "Hey Dad, I thought you said Michael was dead." "Yes," I replied, "We buried him this morning." Ethan then said, "Then who is this cat standing at our back door?" Sure enough, there stood Michael, waiting to come in to eat his breakfast. You guessed it... we buried someone else's cat that morning!

I've told this humorous story dozens of times over the years. I guess the funniest part of the story was that I was so emotional at the burial site, and even spoke words of honor to somebody else's dead cat. You know, we can connect to other people's pain and heartache better when we imagine their pain as our own. Had I not thought the cat I was burying was our cat Michael, no tears would have been shed, and no words of respect would have been spoken. So, here's an interesting challenge for today: Put yourself in the shoes of those around you who are hurting. Minister to them as if their pain is your own. You'll be surprised by how much more effective your ministry to others will be. ***Weep with those who weep (Romans 12:15).***

JESUS HATED???
February 8 | August 8

Here's a question for you: How many times did Jesus say the words, "I hate" in the New Testament? You might be surprised by the answer. As a matter of fact, I'd venture to say that 95% of the people will get this wrong.

The answer is TWO TIMES. Yes, two times Jesus says the words "I hate" in the New Testament. It's written in red letters so there's no mistaking it. If you search through the four gospels, (Matthew, Mark, Luke and John) you won't find it there. So, where else are the words of Jesus recorded in the New Testament? Flip over to the book of Revelation, and you'll find that the first three chapters of Revelation are chock full of the words of Jesus, as He speaks to John on the Isle of Patmos. It is in this discourse you will twice find Jesus saying He hates something.

In Revelation 2:5, Jesus says, "But this thou hast, that thou hatest the deeds of the Nicolaitans, which I ALSO HATE." Further down in the same chapter, in verse 15, Jesus says, "So hast thou also them that hold the doctrine of the Nicolaitans, which thing I HATE." Whoever the Nicolaitans were, there was one thing we know about them for sure: Jesus HATED their DEEDS and their DOCTRINE. I'll say it this way: Jesus HATED their ACTIONS and their TEACHING.

What did the Nicolaitans "do" and "teach"? Most scholars agree that the Nicolaitans practiced sexual immorality, and taught that it was permissible as part of the Christian lifestyle. Their viewpoint and doctrine came from a misunderstanding about the teaching of "grace." Their teaching perverted the truth of God's grace and replaced "freedom FROM sin" with "freedom TO sin." Jesus said that He HATED their deeds and their doctrine. Now, before anybody gets their feathers ruffled, I'll point out that Jesus didn't say He hated the people. He hated their deeds and their doctrines. Jesus is well able to distinguish between people, and their actions. He can love a sinner and hate their sin. He doesn't have a problem saying that He HATES the actions of a sinner. And, more specifically He HATES any teaching that God's people can live a promiscuous lifestyle without any repercussions.

Does it surprise you that Jesus said "I hate"? It did me. After all, we hear all the time that God is LOVE and Jesus is LOVE. So, if Jesus is LOVE but He says He HATES something then I want to LOVE what He LOVES... but I also want to HATE what He HATES... don't you?

FEED THEM
February 9 | August 9

I saw the mailman stop at my neighbor's house. He got out of his mail truck and stepped up to their fence to talk to their dog, Pete. As I looked on I saw him give Pete some treats to eat. He's obviously a dog lover. I thought about how giving food to an animal is the easiest way to instill trust in them, and to show them that you care. Then it hit me like a ton of bricks… we do the same thing with humans. If you really care about someone, the easiest way to show them is by feeding them.

When I was a young man and met my future wife, Lisa, I asked her out on a date. Guys aren't really clever about romance, but one thing we do know for sure is that a girl's got to eat. So, I asked Lisa if she wanted to go out to eat with me. I showed her that I wanted to be with her, and that I cared… by feeding her. Later on, as we became more serious, she invited me over to her apartment where she fixed me the best lemon chicken I'd ever tasted. She was showing me that she cared… by feeding me. And, she's been feeding me ever since!

So, here's an important truth in life… If you care about someone you feed them. Remember when the multitudes came to hear Jesus' teaching and the disciples wanted to send them away so they could get food? Jesus told the disciples, "You feed them." That led to The Feeding of the 5,000.

After His resurrection, Jesus was visiting with His disciples one day and said to Peter, "Peter, do you love Me?" Peter replied, "Yes Lord you know that I love You." Jesus said, "FEED My sheep." He said "FEED My sheep" three times to Peter that day. Jesus wants people to be fed… it's the number one way to show that you care, and that you love… FEED PEOPLE.

Now, you've got to understand that different people have different things that they're hungry for. Some people are hungry for Mexican food, others for steak and potatoes. Likewise, the inner hunger inside people is different. Some are hungry for encouragement, some are hungry for fellowship, some are hungry for acceptance… we all have different hungers within us. Find someone this week who is "hungry"…. and feed them.

Mark 6:36-37(NLT)
"Send the crowds away so they can go to the nearby farms and villages and buy something to eat." But Jesus said, "You FEED them."

THOU ART WITH ME
February 10 | August 10

Years ago, I was taking my daughter and son (who were at the time 8 and 6 years old) on a little walk around our block, holding their hands, enjoying the Sunday evening. The little church on the corner of our street had already started their evening service. We got to the place where we needed to cross the road. We heard a "meowing" from behind us and saw one of our kittens trying to follow us, so after we crossed the road we waited for the kitten to follow.

Just then we heard tires squealing around a corner just down the road from where we were standing. The guy was driving like a maniac, quickly accelerating to a speed of maybe 50 miles per hour, heading our way. The kitten just barely made it across the road before the crazy driver got to where we were standing on the sidewalk. In frustration, I yelled at the driver, "Slow down!" The driver stopped after he passed us, right in the church parking lot, and yelled out, "What did you say Mister?" I said, "Slow down coming through here. You almost ran over our kitten!" The driver replied with a string of expletives that would make a sailor blush... he cussed me out, in front of a church, and even worse yet, in front of two impressionable children. My kids immediately started crying. They were sobbing and pulling on me, saying, "Daddy, let's go back home. We're scared!" I was so upset to see them so visibly distraught.

I guess what upset me the most about that moment in time was not that I got cussed out, but that my kids heard it and didn't feel safe... even though I was standing right there with them. I'll say it again... They didn't feel safe, even though I was standing right there with them. That's the incredible power that evil and darkness has. It has the power to steal your confidence in your Protector and Provider... the one who cares about you more than anyone else in the world.

I think about Jesus, after a long, hard day of ministry, He told His disciples, "Let's get in a boat and go to the other side of the lake." They got in the boat and started their journey. Jesus was so tired that he fell asleep in the back of the boat on a pillow. If you remember this story, you know that a great storm arose, and the disciples thought they were going to drown in it. In total fear and panic, they woke Jesus from His sleep and said, "Master, don't you care that we are about to die?!" Jesus awoke from His sleep, rebuked the wind and waves, and there was a great calm. Then

He said those words of rebuke that almost seemed insensitive to their feelings, "Why is that you are so fearful? Where is your faith?"

Jesus was IN THE BOAT with the disciples, yet they were afraid, as if His presence in the boat was not sufficient reason to be fearless…. to be courageous. The "fear of evil" had so gripped their heart that they questioned Jesus' ability to save them from the darkness of evil that surrounded them. David, the young shepherd boy, understood the power of God's presence when he said, "Yea, though I walk through the valley of the shadow of death, I WILL FEAR NO EVIL… FOR THOU ART WITH ME." This is where the children of Father God get their confidence… in knowing that God is with them. If He's standing by my side, (or even sleeping in the boat that I'm in) there's no reason for me to be afraid.

Why are you fearful today? Is God with you or is He not? If you know the correct answer, fear will become a thing of the past.

Romans 8:31 (NIV)
If God is for us, who can be against us?

I LOVE YOU… AND I'M PROUD OF YOU!
February 11 | August 11

There are two things that everyone needs to hear spoken to them during their lifetime… "I love you, and I'm proud of you." Kids need to hear it from their parents. Wives need to hear it from their husbands. Friends need to hear it from their friends. We all need to know that someone loves us, and that they're pleased with us.

Now, sometimes it's easier to say the first part than the second part. I mean, I can say "I love you" to you, even when you've been a real "stinker." But for me to say "I'm proud of you" means that you've done something, or that you've acted in a certain way, that pleases me. So, my love for you is based on WHO I AM, but my being proud of you is based on WHO YOU ARE.

What is the absolute best thing you will ever hear God say to you? He said it to Jesus at His baptism… "This is my beloved Son (I love you) in whom I am well-pleased (I'm proud of you)." I would love to hear God say those same words to me. But I understand, the "I love you" part is up to Him, while the "I'm proud of you" part is up to me.

DOCUMENTED
February 12 | August 12

Revelation 20:15 (KJV)
And whosoever was not found written in the book of life was cast into the lake of fire.

There is a book in Heaven. It is called "The Book of Life." Do you know if your name is in it? God keeps documented proof of who belongs to Him in the book. So, please take this in the way it is intended… not political… just truth… There are no "undocumented" aliens in Heaven.

God doesn't let anyone into Heaven unless they meet His requirements. There are proper steps one must take to become a resident of Heaven. Have you taken the necessary steps? God will not make exceptions. You will not get "grand-fathered" in. Each person must confess with their mouth "Jesus is Lord" and believe in their heart that God raised Jesus from the dead (Romans 10:9-10), if they want their name to be found in the Book of Life.

The book of Revelation says that people from "every nation, tribe and tongue" will be there. NO ONE will be excluded because of race, color, national origin or age. The only ones who will be excluded are those who did not take the time to become a citizen of Heaven while living on Earth.

Jesus said "You must be born again." Being born the first time made you a citizen of Earth… being "born again" makes you a citizen of Heaven. It's that simple. If you haven't already, get DOCUMENTED today!

PRAISE SILENCES THE FOE

The greatest thing you will ever do in this life is give praise to God. So, the greatest victory Satan will ever have in your life is to keep you from praising God. If he can't steal your praise, he can't be victorious in your life. Give God praise today no matter what is happening in your life and you will always have a note of victory over the devil.

Psalm 8:2 (NIV)
Through the praise of children and infants you have established a strong-hold against your enemies, to silence the foe and the avenger.

WHAT'S YOUR PASSION?
February 13 | August 13

Out of curiosity, I looked up the origin of the word "compassion." It comes from two Latin words:

> **com** - *meaning "with"*
> **pati** - *meaning "to suffer."*

So, when you say you have compassion for someone, you're actually saying that you're "suffering with" that person. Isn't it interesting that the word PASSION means "to suffer"? When you read about the PASSION of the Christ you understand that we're talking about the things He suffered through, leading to His death.

I think it's odd, and almost sort of funny, that today we use the word PASSION like it's some kind of mystical feeling that you have inside that drives you to your destiny. We say things like, "What's your passion in life?" or "Follow your passion."

With the understanding that PASSION means "to suffer," think again about the way we use the word PASSION in our modern day. "What's your PASSION in life" would mean "What do you suffer for in life." Your calling in life is not necessarily something that gives you goosebumps and warm fuzzies. More accurately, it is something that you're so desirous to do that it hurts... the thought of NOT doing it feels like suffering... and you'd do it no matter what kind of pain you experienced in the process of pursuing it.

Where did we get off thinking PASSION is a warm, cozy, bubbly feeling on the inside? I don't understand how it has gotten so twisted from its original meaning.

MY PRAYER FOR TODAY:
"Lord, renew PASSION within each of us. A passion that is willing to suffer for what we strongly believe in. Forgive our misinterpretation of the word. Help us regain its proper meaning and impact. When things are difficult and painful, but we're doing what you've called us to do, give us strength to follow through to the end... just as Christ did during His PASSION for us."

THAT'S EXCESSIVE!
February 14 | August 14

After Billy Graham's death, I saw where people were criticizing the amount of money spent on his funeral. Someone suggested that Billy Graham would not have approved. Others suggested that not even God would approve. Why do people do that? Why do people suppose that there is some kind of price that is too excessive when it comes to God's kingdom, His church or His people? Whenever I hear of people doing that, my mind immediately goes to Jesus' last days on earth when Mary poured expensive perfume on Jesus' feet and Judas complained that the perfume should have been sold, and the money given to the poor instead of being "wasted" on Jesus' feet. When people complain about the cost of things used for God's people or His kingdom they are aligning themselves with Judas Iscariot (who, by the way, wasn't concerned about the poor, but only cared about the cost of the perfume because he was Jesus' treasurer, and used to steal from the moneybag).

Does God care about how much things cost? When the temple was being built in the Old Testament, God instructed that its furnishing be made of gold and silver. Sounds a little excessive doesn't it?! Could you imagine if a church today had pulpits and pews constructed of gold? What a scandalous thing that would be for the news networks to report about! Did God not think that was excessive, using the most precious and valuable metal to build with? To answer that question, just think about what the streets in Heaven are paved with! God paves the streets with gold in Heaven… "God, that's excessive!"

You've heard the story of the widow's mite, haven't you? Jesus saw the rich folks putting money in the temple treasury, but His eye was drawn to a poor widow who put in two mites. Jesus said, "this poor widow put in all that she had." Again, could you imagine the scandal that would be today, for a preacher to let a poor widow give her entire savings into the church collection plate? Shouldn't Jesus have stopped that lady from giving all her money to "the church"? "The church should have been giving money to the poor widow, not the other way around." That's what most people would have said.

God doesn't complain about the cost of things… and I'm glad. You see, one day God gave His most costly, most expensive gift to the world. He gave Jesus as a sacrifice for our sins. Personally, I think He spent WAY TOO MUCH on us. The price was excessive! But, I'm a child of God today because God gave His very best, and most precious, so that I, a poor sinner, could be an heir to His kingdom.

Thank you God, for being so excessive in your love for us!

THE ILLUSION OF DEATH
February 15 | August 15

During the harsh months of winter, I observed a frail little fruit tree. Its barren limbs were lightly covered with frost. It inspired me to write this poem of encouragement to all who are experiencing a season of barrenness.

As long as life courses through my veins
I will not give up or surrender.
Even through the harshest winters,
Even when the skies remain gray for days on end.
I may look barren and dead,
But make no mistake
Life still flows inside of me.
Winter will soon be ending.
Spring is coming.
You will see me bloom soon,
And you will completely forget
That I once looked so barren and frail.
There was something in my roots,
Something you couldn't see.
It helped me hold on through the harshest times,
It fed me when the ground around me was hard and frozen.
Yes, soon I will be green with life,
I will bear flowers, and even fruit.
The Giver of Life has given His promise.
Dreary days will end,
The sun will shine,
The season of barrenness will subside,
And the world will once again be reminded
That life will always be victorious
Over the illusion of death.

FIX THE DOOR
February 16 | August 16

I'm not at all proud to admit this, but in the heat of an angry moment, I stormed through my house and slammed the bedroom door behind me. (He that is without sin among you, let him cast the first stone.) After I cooled down a bit and came to my senses, several hours later, I repented of my immature behavior and asked the Lord for forgiveness.

The next day, when I went to the bedroom and tried to close the door, it wouldn't shut properly. I thought that was odd. I had to jiggle the knob and lean against the door to get it to latch. I didn't think any more about it until the next day when I tried to shut the door again and met with the same problem. I opened the door to see what the problem was. I discovered that the door facing was broken. Yes, my outburst of anger proved fatal... I broke my door! When I realized what had happened, I said to myself, "Well, that's what you get for losing your cool!" So I just dealt with the problem.

For the next couple of weeks, every time I tried to close that door I was reminded of my sin, and the consequences, thereof. Every time I'd jiggle that door knob and lean against the door to shut it, I was humbled by the thought of how immature I can be... how sinful I can be. I guess, in a way, I needed that constant reminder. It kind of "put me in my place," if you know what I mean. We should never get comfortable with our sin and just accept it, so I guess that door was a good attention-getter for me.

But, you know what? After a full month of having to jiggle the door knob, and lean against the door to fully shut it, I began to get aggravated. Sure, it was a good reminder of my sin, and how I need to get better self control, but ultimately, I had a broken door that needed to be fixed. So one day, I just stopped everything I was doing for an hour or so. I got a hammer and a screwdriver and pulled that door facing apart, adjusted the locking mechanism and fixed my broken door. It had become more than a constant reminder of my sin and my need for forgiveness... it had become a constant irritation.

It's true that we need occasional reminders of our propensity to sin. But life is no fun when you have constant reminders of your defeats and failures in front of you all the time. Those continual reminders become an irritation. That irritation is designed to lead you to a cure... fix the problem. Don't live a broken life and constantly confess that you're a messed up individual. Self-loathing doesn't change who you are and it doesn't make you better. But, if you'll take the necessary steps to make adjustments in your life, and seek God's help and counsel, you can overcome your past failures and defeats.

Fix the door!

UN-RIGHT
February 17 | August 17

"If we confess our sins, He is faithful and just to forgive us our sins, and cleanse us from all unrighteousness." 1 John 1:9 (KJV)

Two things happen when we confess to God that we have sinned (or have done wrong).

1. God forgives us of the sin
2. He cleanses us from unrighteousness.

So what is "Unrighteousness"? Take a close look at the word. Look at it like this: "Unright - eousness." It's being "unright," or a better word is just plain and simple WRONG. Do you realize you need to be cleansed from WRONG in your life? Not just forgiven, but cleansed. So, if you never confess that you are WRONG you can't be cleansed from your WRONG.

That's the problem we're dealing with in today's society. No one will admit or confess that they are WRONG. They say, "God loves me the way I am" and that is true. He loves us even when we're WRONG. But until we confess that we're WRONG we can't be made RIGHT. I want to be RIGHT. Not so I can look good or have people admire me. I want to be RIGHT because that's what God is. HE IS RIGHT-EOUS.

MY PRAYER FOR TODAY:
"Lord, as I confess my sins, cleanse me from all unrighteousness. I want to be made RIGHT and I know that will only happen when I humbly admit that I've been WRONG."

MILK AND HONEY
February 18 | August 18

Throughout the Old Testament, the Promised Land is described as "a land flowing with milk and honey" which signifies that it's a land of provision and abundance. Let me show you a couple of verses that might add some light to this "milk and honey" concept.

1 Peter 2:2
As newborn babes, desire the sincere MILK of the WORD, that ye may grow thereby

Revelation 10:10
And I took the little book out of the angel's hand, and ate it up; and it was in my mouth sweet as HONEY

Notice that God's Word/s are described as both MILK and HONEY in these two verses in the New Testament.

The provision of God awaits all those who seek the Promised Land. It is a land that flows with MILK and HONEY. It is a land that flows with the WORD OF GOD. Everything you need in life is found in the Word of God. He makes provision for you by giving you His Word. Speak His Word over your life daily… it will nourish you like milk… it will make life sweeter as well, just like honey. God's Word is where God's provision is found. Take it…. and eat it… and drink it.

Matthew 5:6 (NIV)
Blessed are those who hunger and thirst for righteousness, for they will be filled.

INSTANT FAILURE

Success will take time...
Failure will take time...
Quitting takes no time at all.
Quitting is INSTANT FAILURE.

Galatians 6:9 (NIV)
Let us not become weary in doing good, for at the proper time we will reap a harvest if we DO NOT GIVE UP.

ADAM'S RIB
February 19 | August 19

So many of the questions we have in life can be answered simply by going back to the origin of things as they are revealed in the book of Genesis. Take, for instance, the idea of "loneliness."

God had created a great big Earth and everything in it, and after all His work was finished He saw that it was VERY GOOD (Genesis 1:31). But then, only one chapter over, we hear God say "It is NOT GOOD for man to be alone" (Genesis 2:18). If you're alone and lonely, I want to tell you that God sees it, and He doesn't think it's good for you to be lonely. You might say "Thanks a lot Greg...but that doesn't take the loneliness away!" But let's take a look at the rest of the story.

God didn't just say "It's not GOOD for man to be alone," He also did something to remedy the situation. And, here is where we find part of the answer to combating loneliness. You see, God didn't just bring SOMEBODY to Adam. He actually took SOMETHING out of Adam so that Adam wouldn't be alone anymore. He took a rib OUT of Adam and formed it into a woman… into Eve… and then Adam wasn't lonely anymore.

So, this is what we learn from this: God oftentimes REQUIRES something OUT of us to overcome loneliness… we may have to GIVE UP or SURRENDER a part of who we are for the transaction to be completed.

If you're lonely today maybe God wants to take something out of you and fashion it into the answer to your loneliness. It could be extreme shyness… it could be low self-esteem… it could be your personal comfort zone… it could even be your quest for the "perfect person." (Yes, Eve was the perfect person but you know the rest of the story, right?) I don't know your situation, but I know my God, and I know the way He does things. He showed us in Genesis chapter 2. So, if you're lonely, and don't want to be, ask God what He would like to take out of you in order to fashion it into the answer to your prayers.

Genesis 2:22 (KJV)
And the rib, which the Lord God had taken from man, made he a woman, and brought her unto the man.

EXPEL THE PERPETRATOR
February 20 | August 20

I was asked to pray for a group of six men… that God would bring unity among them. Seems like a reasonable request, doesn't it? They didn't ask for 1,000 people to come together in unity, and not even 100… just six individuals. How hard can that be?! Yet, it's very difficult to achieve unity with even as few as six individuals when all six have their own upbringing, personal viewpoints, and likes and dislikes. When this prayer request was shared I immediately thought of this verse from the book of Amos:

Amos 3:3 (KJV)
Can two walk together, except they be agreed?

Nothing can be achieved among a group of people without unity and agreement. Just two people… they can't even WALK together without agreement and unity. Think about it. There has to be an agreement about the distance that will be travelled, the rate of speed that will be used, the final destination, and the path that will be taken.

There is disunity and disharmony in larger organizations like businesses, corporations, churches and government, but there's also disunity in smaller groups like families, ball teams, and even friendships.

Some people don't like the fact that there can be disunity even in church. I've seen it first hand. It's no uglier than the disunity you find anywhere else, but it's still ugly. Think about where the very first mention of disunity happened, though. It happened in a blissful, holy place called Heaven when one arrogant angel thought that he deserved greater attention than God. You know the rest of the story… there was disunity in Heaven and the perpetrator was expelled, along with those who joined forces with him.

Listen, anytime and any place you find disunity I can guarantee you who is behind it… the original instigator of disunity. Until there is agreement about the cause of disunity, and people purpose to only bring accusations against him, disunity will always continue. But when disunity is conquered and the culprit who instigated it is removed, Jesus says "Truly I tell you that if TWO of you on earth AGREE about anything they ask for, it will be done for them by my Father in heaven" (Matthew 18:19).

There is great power in agreement… even with just two people. Satan knows it. That's why he works so hard to bring division. Purpose in your heart not to let his tactics work in your life. Expose the thief who is causing discord and disunity in your life and among the people you work with and fellowship with. Don't blame people… blame the source... then do what God did in Heaven.... EXPEL THE PERPETRATOR.

2 Corinthians 2:11 (NAS)
So that no advantage would be taken of us by Satan, for we are not ignorant of his schemes.

"WITH" GOD
February 21 | August 21

An angel came to Mary and announced the news that she would give birth to a son. When Mary asked Gabriel how she would be able to have a child when she was a virgin, he went into detail telling how the event would take place. Then, he said something that is often quoted… and also often misquoted. In Luke 1:37, Gabriel says, "For nothing will be impossible WITH God." It DOES NOT say, "For nothing will be impossible FOR God."

I don't know why it took me so long to see this, but this scripture verse leapt off the page when I read it in church one Sunday morning. The difference that a preposition makes is incredible! I suppose everybody believes and agrees that nothing is impossible FOR God. God is powerful and can do unimaginable things. But the question we need to ask ourselves is this: Do we believe that nothing is impossible WITH God?

The word WITH means "accompanied by another person or thing."

So, when we say "Nothing is impossible WITH God," we're inferring that He is accompanying us, or, that we are accompanying Him. And, when that is the case, there are no impossibilities in our lives. That's why I'm glad to be in a relationship WITH Him. He accompanies me, and I accompany Him… so, nothing is impossible for ME when I am being accompanied by HIM!

Psalm 60:12 (NIV)
WITH God we will gain the victory, and he will trample down our enemies.

"WHO IS MY NEIGHBOR?"
February 22 | August 22

A religious man came to Jesus and said, "What must I do to inherit eternal life?" Jesus said to the man, "What does the scripture say?" The man replied, "Love the Lord your God with all your heart, soul, strength and mind, and love your neighbor as yourself." Jesus said, "You've answered correctly. Do this and you shall live." (Paraphrase of Luke 10:25-28). Now, the scripture says that this man felt the need to justify himself by asking one more question. So, he asked Jesus, "And who is my neighbor?" In essence he was asking, "Define what you mean by the word 'neighbor.'"

In response to this question Jesus gives us his famous parable known as "The Good Samaritan." In the story of the Good Samaritan a Jewish man was beaten up by thieves and left for dead. In a short period of time, two separate individuals (both Jews) passed by the man who was left for dead, but did nothing to help him. Then a Samaritan (a hated enemy of the Jews) came upon the fallen man and helped him, and took care of him. After telling the story Jesus asked the religious man, "Who do you think was neighbor to the man who was beaten by the thieves?" The man replied, "The one who showed him mercy." Jesus replied, "Go and do likewise."

"WHO IS MY NEIGHBOR?" It's important to know the answer to that question. Is it just the person who lives next door to you? The Greek word "neighbor" in this passage is the word PLESION which means "near." The first part of the word NEIGHBOR is NEIGH or NIGH, so it's somebody who is close by, or NIGH to you. But, Jesus shows us in this story that anytime you're NEAR another person you have become their neighbor for that moment in time. They don't have to LIVE next door to you… they just have to be ALIVE next to you during your daily journey of life.

So, when you're in the grocery store, every person you pass by in the aisle becomes your neighbor for a brief moment. When you're sitting at a restaurant and someone sits in the booth next to you, they become your neighbor. When you're at the gym working out and someone gets on the treadmill next to you, they become your neighbor. We come into contact with hundreds of people each day who qualify as our neighbors, according to Jesus' words. Do we love them as we love ourselves? If they need help, do we offer them a hand?

Jesus shows us that our neighbors aren't just the people in our neighborhood. Neighborhoods can separate people. They separate rich people from poor people. They separate ethnicities. They separate age groups. But with Jesus' definition of NEIGHBOR we come to understand that our neighbors are the people all around us in our daily lives. Those who show mercy to those who are in need are the best examples of NEIGHBORS that can be found. The Good Samaritan is the prime example of this.

James 2:8 (NAS)
If, however, you are fulfilling the royal law according to the Scripture, "YOU SHALL LOVE YOUR NEIGHBOR AS YOURSELF," you are doing well.

JESUS OF NAZARETH
February 23 | August 23

Almost everybody knows the story of the baby Jesus, born in Bethlehem, but we know very little about his childhood and early years. One thing we know for sure is that He spent most of his growing-up years in a town called Nazareth. Now, Nazareth was not a town that had a very good reputation. We know this because when Phillip told Nathaniel that he had found the Messiah and his name was "Jesus of Nazareth," Nathaniel replied with, "Can anything good come from Nazareth?" (John 1:46) Nazareth was not a well-known town like Bethlehem. It didn't have any history to speak of (the Jewish historian, Josephus, doesn't even mention it in his writings). It was ridiculed by other neighboring cities and villages and was probably used as a byword – as the butt of jokes, even. But, the history of Nazareth and the reputation that it had held for decades (and centuries, most likely) changed all because of one very important person who "put it on the map"… Jesus of Nazareth. As a matter of fact, Jesus is called "Jesus of Nazareth" seventeen times in the New Testament.

Not only did Nazareth get a reputation boost when Jesus walked on this earth, but after His death, resurrection and ascension, Jesus' followers became known as "the sect of the Nazarenes" (Acts 24:5). That may sound familiar to you since there is a Christian denomination called "The Church of the Nazarene" to this day.

So, what can we glean from this? Here's what I see… Jesus can make his home in a place that has a bad reputation and give it a good reputation. Yes, all Jesus has to do in order to change the reputation of a place (or a person) is just live there. Does He live in you?

GOD "BUILDS" ON WORDS
February 24 | August 24

Matthew 7:24 (NIV)
"Therefore everyone who hears these WORDS of Mine and acts on them, may be compared to a wise man who BUILT his house on the rock."

Notice the two capitalized words in the scripture verse above. Jesus is inferring in this verse that people should BUILD their lives upon His WORDS. Keeping this in mind, when Peter told Jesus, "You are the Christ, the Son of the Living God" Jesus replied with, "Upon this rock I will BUILD my church." It was not Peter (the person) that Jesus built his church upon... it was Peter's WORDS "You are the Christ." You see, GOD BUILDS ON WORDS.

Think about it. How did He BUILD the world? He spoke WORDS. To create light, He said, "Let there be light." Genesis 1:9-10 says, "And God said, 'Let the waters under the heaven be gathered together unto one place, and let the dry land appear' and it was so. And God called the dry land Earth; and the gathering together of the waters called he Seas." God SPOKE creation into existence. He created and built using WORDS. Hebrews says, "By faith we understand that the worlds were framed [just like a house is framed by a carpenter] by the WORD of God" (Hebrews 11:3).

So, if God BUILDS things by using WORDS, think about the building materials that you are giving Him today to work with. The WORDS coming from your mouth are the building materials of your life. Negative, critical and judgemental words will not build anything that is lasting or beautiful. Positive, encouraging, faith-filled, hope-filled words are the kinds of WORDS God loves to use in His BUILDING program. As a matter of fact, the word EDIFY means "to build up." It comes from the Greek word "oikodome" which literally means "to be a house-builder." Are you an "edifier"? Are you building up?

What are you building with your words?

MY PRAYER FOR TODAY:
"Lord, help me keep a guard on my mouth. Let only positive, encouraging, edifying words come from my lips... words that You would be happy to BUILD upon."

A RESURRECTING BREATH
February 25 | August 25

I was just about to enter the door of the church on a cold Autumn morning when I saw a lifeless lizard lying on the doorway steps. When I first saw him I assumed he was dead... frozen from the extreme cold of the previous night. His body was a blackish brown and he was stiff and cold. When I picked him up to avoid stepping on him, I noticed that he moved slightly. The little fellow was frozen stiff, but he was still alive. So I held him in my hand for a short time and within a minute or so I detected more life coming into his body (I guess the warmth of my hand thawed him out some). So, I cupped my hands together, and then exhaled inside my hands to cover him with warm moisture. That one breath awakened him and he started wiggling around inside my cupped hands. He was "resurrected" from the dead.

I thought about that moment in the Bible, after Jesus was resurrected from the dead, when he appeared to His disciples, and breathed on them and said, "Receive ye the Holy Spirit." Something happened during that transaction that we don't fully understand. You see, before that moment, in God's eyes, mankind was dead... hard and cold... lifeless... no sign of spiritual life within. Sure, they were physically alive, but in God's eyes spiritual life is what makes a person "really alive." Do you remember that Adam was just a lump of clay (with a physical body) but the Bible says that when God BREATHED on him, that's when Adam became "alive." Man needs the breath of God to be spiritually alive. Going to church, reading the Bible, and praying are all worthwhile spiritual endeavors, but until a person receives God's breath into their life they're just as cold, stiff and lifeless in God's eyes as that lizard was in my eyes.

I'll ask you an important question, then. Have you been resurrected from the dead by the breath of Jesus Christ?

Ezekiel 37:8-10 (NAS)
And I looked, and behold, sinews were on them, and flesh grew and skin covered them; but there was no breath in them. Then He said to me, "Prophesy to the breath, prophesy, son of man, and say to the breath, 'Thus says the Lord GOD, "Come from the four winds, O breath, and breathe on these slain, that they come to life."' So I prophesied as He commanded me, and the breath came into them, and they came to life and stood on their feet, an exceedingly great army

PURITY
February 26 | August 26

"To the pure, all things are pure, but to those who are corrupted and do not believe, nothing is pure. In fact, both their minds and consciences are corrupted." Titus 1:15 (NIV)

Here's a question for you: Do you believe that purity exists? Titus tells us that corrupted and unbelieving people believe "nothing is pure" but pure people see purity everywhere they look. Jesus said, "Blessed are the PURE in heart, for they shall see God" (Matthew 5:8). Pure people want to see God, so they look for the good. No doubt they also notice the bad, but that is not their focus. They know if they want to see God they'll need to focus on the good... because God is good, so He can be found "in the good." Listen, if you're focusing on the bad and negative that's going on in the world it will affect you, without a doubt. It will make you skeptical and critical... it will make you believe that "no thing" and "no one" is pure, it will make you take your eyes off of God (the One who is found "in the good"). But, pure people see through different eyes. They see purity all around them. They see the good around them... they see God around them.

Proverbs 22:11 (NAS) - He who loves purity of heart and whose speech is gracious, the king is his friend.

THE SEEN AND THE UNSEEN

I was talking to a friend about "spiritual" things when my friend said, "People don't talk much about spiritual things because it doesn't seem REAL to them." I laughed and agreed with him and said, "The funny thing about it is that God is a Spirit (spiritual), and He created everything we see. So Someone who is 'unseen' created everything that is 'seen.' Now if the 'unseen' created the 'seen,' then it stands to reason that the 'unseen' is more real than the 'seen,' just as surely as the 'creator' is more real than the 'created.' So, this is what it boils down to: the things we see, that we call 'real' are really less 'real' than the things which are unseen that we call 'unreal.'" (Mind explosion!)

This is the reason the Bible tells us:
"Walk by faith, not by SIGHT" (2 Corinthians 5:7).

A HOLE IN MY POCKET
February 27 | August 27

I had a dream one night that I completely forgot about... until I came upon a lost dollar bill on my walk the next morning. I picked up the dollar bill. It was drenched with dew, so I knew it had been laying there all night. As I walked along further, that's when the forgotten dream was remembered. You see, in my dream I was walking with a friend along a pathway. I had a dollar bill in my pocket and when I reached in to get it, I discovered it was missing. I looked back on the path I was walking on and saw it back behind me. I went and picked it up, stuck it back in my pocket and continued walking on the path. I reached into my pocket once more. The dollar bill was missing. I thought to myself, "How did that dollar bill just disappear?" I looked back on the trail and there it was behind me, again. I picked the dollar bill up, put it back in my pocket and then discovered the cause for its continued disappearance... there was a big, gaping hole in the bottom of my pocket. And, just like that, the dream was over.

As I thought about how strange of a coincidence it was that I discovered a lost dollar bill the following morning, I couldn't help but wonder if there was some kind of message in this dream. It was then that I remembered this passage of scripture found in Haggai:

"You earn wages, only to put them in a purse with holes in it. This is what the Lord Almighty says: "Give careful thought to your ways. Go up into the mountains and bring down timber and build my house, so that I may take pleasure in it and be honored," says the Lord. "You expected much, but see, it turned out to be little. What you brought home, I blew away. Why?" declares the Lord Almighty. "Because of my house, which remains a ruin, while each of you is busy with your own house." Haggai 1:6-9 (NIV)

What a convicting word! In this scripture, God is telling His people that they were more concerned about their own homes and their business than about God's house and His business. As a result He withheld His blessing from them to get their attention... so they could see their misplaced priorities. That's why it seemed like they were putting their money into purses with holes in them.

MY PRAYER FOR TODAY:
"Lord, help me to put YOUR house before MY house. Bless my finances as I determine in my heart to seek Your kingdom first!"

SPIT OUT THE BITTERNESS
February 28 | August 28

I picked up a few dozen pecans on my morning walk and cracked several, and ate them as I walked along. They were sweet and delicious. After eating about 5 or 6 I told myself inwardly, "Okay, this is your last one" and I shelled one last pecan and popped it in my mouth. As I chewed on that final pecan I discovered that it was very bitter, so I quickly spit the pieces from my mouth. I couldn't stand having that bitter taste in my mouth, especially having just eaten a half dozen really tasty, sweet pecans. Even though I told myself that was my last pecan for the morning, I broke my vow, and shelled one last pecan and ate it… it was delicious. I couldn't let my final experience be a bitter one.

Bitterness steals away your memory of sweetness (and I'm not just talking about pecans now). There are people who have wonderful memories of sweet friendships that ended bitterly, so the sweet memories are shrouded by the bitterness. I'm amazed by how many families have been broken up, brothers and sisters not talking to each other, simply because there was one bitter moment that brought an end to all the sweetness. Some hold on to the unforgiveness their whole life and go to their graves with the "bitter taste" in their mouths.

Almost everyone has gone through some kind of relationship issue that ended bitterly. It is an unfortunate fact of life. If the last taste you had of friendship and meaningful relationship left you with a "bitter taste in your mouth" determine that you'll not let things end that way. There is a sweetness in life that will only be discovered when you spit out the bitterness, and get it completely out of your system. One day we will all stand before the Lord… we'll breathe our last breath here on this planet. Don't let your last taste of life end with bitterness!

Hebrews 12:15 (NAS)
See to it that no one comes short of the grace of God; that no root of bitterness springing up causes trouble, and by it many be defiled;

Psalm 34:8 (NIV)
Taste and see that the LORD is good; blessed is the one who takes refuge in him.

WHERE ARE YOU BEING PULLED?
March 1 | August 29

The word *tract* is the root word of these three words: attract, distract and subtract. *Tract* comes from a Latin words which means "to pull, or draw."

I shared this information with a group of guys at the Men's Home Bible Study one Monday night. I then told them, "God has a level that he wants you to achieve in life. He's 'pulling' and 'drawing' you to that place... He's ATTRACTING you. At the same time, this world is also 'pulling' you and 'drawing' you AWAY from what God is calling you to... it is DIS-TRACTING you from the level He wants you to achieve."

As I was sharing this, one of the guys got up from the table and left the room for a minute. I wondered what was going on. He went to another room and turned off a television that had been left on. When he came back I thanked him for helping illustrate the meaning of the word DIS-TRACT. You see, as I was teaching this lesson, that television was "pull-ing on" everyone in that room who was trying to listen to me. I even admitted that it had "pulled on" me and made it difficult to concentrate on what I was sharing. In humorous fashion, I stood up and acted as if the television was pulling me toward it. I couldn't have asked for a better illustration! Basically, instead of being in the room where the Bible Study was, we were being "pulled" into the adjacent room where the television was blaring. That's what worldly DISTRACTIONS do... they "pull us" away from the place God wants us to be.

Then we moved on to the last word: SUBTRACT. The prefix "sub" means "below." It's bad enough that this world is pulling us AWAY from the place God wants us to be, but we also have a spiritual enemy who wants to "pull us" BELOW God's desired place for us... the devil wants to SUB-TRACT from our lives!

So, putting all this together we understand this: God is ATTRACTING US to a higher place in life... He wants us to experience success and blessing. This world is DISTRACTING us from that higher place and pulling us toward the things this world has to offer (which are on a much lower level than what God has for us). All the while, the devil is trying to SUBTRACT from us, pulling us to levels even lower than this world offers us, and ulti-mately desiring to "pull us" to his eternal destination... Hell.

THE FAITHFUL
March 2 | August 30

Here's to all the faithful
To the ones who never quit
To those who "take a stand"
Even when they'd rather sit.

They're the ones we all can count on
In highest height or lowest pit.
They're the few who know the meaning
Of the forgotten word COMMIT.

Psalm 31:23 (KJV)
O love the LORD, all you His godly ones!
The LORD preserves the faithful

BE A FINISHER

There's a lot of inspiration, fun and excitement involved in STARTING, but FINISHING is where the reward is. BE A FINISHER! Here are a few scriptures to bring encouragement about FINISHING what you've started.

Luke 14:28-30 (KJV)
For which of you, intending to build a tower, sitteth not down first, and counteth the cost, whether he have sufficient to FINISH it? Otherwise, if he lays the foundation and is unable to FINISH the work, everyone who sees it will ridicule him, saying, 'This man could not FINISH what he started....'

John 4:34 (KJV)
My meat is to do the will of him that sent me, and to FINISH his work.

Ecclesiastes 7:8 (NLT)
FINISHING is better than starting.

2 Timothy 4:7 (NIV)
I have fought the good fight, I have FINISHED the race,
I have kept the faith.

John 19:30 (NIV)
It is FINISHED!

AWAKEN THE DISCOVERER WITHIN
March 3 | August 31

Evidently I woke my dog, Archie, too early one summer morning. As we were taking our morning walk, he was dragging along behind me. He stopped a few times and looked back towards our house as if to say, "Can I just go back to bed?" We were too far along to turn back, so I figured I'd try to motivate him a little bit. "Let's go find a rabbit," I said with an enthusiastic tone of voice. His tail started wagging, his head turned to the direction of our destination, and he trotted out in front of me like his usual self. Sometimes you just need a little motivation to get your day started, and there's no better motivation than "discovery"... to find something that you've been searching for, or longing for.

In Jeremiah 29:13 God says, "And ye shall seek Me, and find Me, when ye shall search for Me with all your heart." Some people have trouble finding motivation in life. When the alarm clock rings they hit the snooze button... several times. But, there is in the heart of every living person a desire to "discover".... to search for hidden things. God, in a sense, has hidden Himself in an attempt to awaken the "discoverer" within all of us. He knows how we love the challenge of searching for hidden things. A few times, I have posted photos on social media of an open field with a rabbit hidden in the picture. It's always interesting to me to see the number of people who like searching for things that are hidden. When we discover hidden things we get a feeling of accomplishment and success.

So, think about it today. Are you having a hard time finding motivation in your life? Do you just want to go back to bed? Or, are you motivated to seek God, to search for Him with ALL YOUR HEART until you find Him? He will put a spring in your step. He will let you find hints and clues to life as you seek Him daily. He will let you discover the treasures that have been hidden from the lazy and the slothful. He will reveal Himself and His kingdom to the diligent ones who don't give up in their search.

Jeremiah 33:3 (English Standard Version)
Call to me and I will answer you, and will tell you great and hidden things that you have not known.'

Deuteronomy 29:29 (NIV)
The secret things belong to the LORD our God, but the things revealed belong to us and to our children forever.

WALK THROUGH IT
March 4 | September 1

The difficulty you're facing is not something that you're supposed to get comfortable with. Nor are you supposed to sit down in the middle of your trials and succumb to them. What does the scripture repeatedly tell the believer to do when they are in the middle of trouble and trials? WALK THROUGH IT! Check out these encouraging verses of scripture.

"Yea, though I WALK THROUGH the valley of the shadow of death I will fear no evil." Psalm 23:4 (KJV)

"When they WALK THROUGH the Valley of Weeping, it will become a place of refreshing springs." Psalm 84:6 (NLT)

"When you pass through the waters, I will be with you; And through the rivers, they will not overflow you. When you WALK THROUGH the fire, you will not be scorched, Nor will the flame burn you." Isaiah 43:2 (NAS)

"You divided the sea for your people so they could WALK THROUGH on dry land!" Nehemiah 9:11 (NLT)

"When His lamp shone over my head, And by His light I WALKED THROUGH darkness." Job 29:3 (NIV)

KEEP ON WALKING CHILD OF GOD!

WHO DOES GOD USE?

God doesn't use the offendable for they're not dependable and are rarely bendable. No, He does something more viable and uses the pliable, because they're so reliable. He uses the stretchable, whose hearts are etchable. He's not looking for the capable, but for the shapeable, because they're unbreakable, and completely unshakeable. They will achieve the unachievable, because they believe the unbelievable.

Isaiah 64:8 (NIV)
Yet you, LORD, are our Father. We are the clay, you are the potter; we are all the work of your hand.

6:33 … 10:33
March 5 | September 2

In my previous book, *My Morning Walks With God I*, I mentioned that I quite frequently see the numbers 6:33 when I check my watch or iPhone. That number reminds me of Matthew 6:33, "Seek ye first the kingdom of God and His righteousness and all these things will be added unto you." Whenever I see those numbers it's like a friendly reminder from the Lord to seek God's kingdom first as I'm going about my daily routine.

Well, recently I've been having a similar thing happen with the numbers 10:33. It seems like every time I turn around to check the clock it's 10:33. After seeing this number pop up more than a couple dozen times in recent weeks I decided to check the scriptures for a passage that coincides with this number. I'll be honest… I was hoping the scripture I'd find was a word of encouragement. I tried my best to find a "10:33" that was uplifting and promising, but this is the one that I really felt like God was trying to get me to see:

Matthew 10:33 - "But whoever denies me before men, I also will deny before my Father who is in heaven."

Today I may look down at my watch and see those familiar numbers again… 6:33… my gentle reminder to seek God's kingdom at all times. But, before this week is over I'm certain I will also see 10:33, and it won't be a "gentle" reminder. No, it will be a kick in the seat of my pants. Yes, it will be a strong warning from the throne of God for me to not deny Christ before men. I can't be afraid of what people think of me when I stand up for Christ, His kingdom, or His cause. HIS perception of me is far more important to me than what a human being thinks of me. If I've pleased Him, but displeased people by doing so, there will be no apology. Yet, even as I make this public profession, I'm reminded of the apostle Peter who made his bold profession of allegiance to the Lord… "I will never deny you, Lord!" How quickly he ended up regretting making such a bold statement!

MY PRAYER FOR TODAY:
"Lord, help me to be strong for You… to not deny You with my words or my actions… to stay faithful to You even if all around me turn away. In Jesus' name I pray. Amen."

AT THE DINNER TABLE WITH GOD
March 6 | September 3

Inside the Old Testament tabernacle there was a table called "The Table of Shewbread." It was separated from the Holy of Holies (where God's presence dwelt) by a thick veil / curtain. The Table of Shewbread had 12 loaves of unleavened bread sitting on it along with other utensils for eating and drinking. The 12 loaves of bread were symbolic of the 12 tribes of Israel. The bread sat there for one whole week, and at the end of the week the old bread would be eaten by the priests and new bread would take its place. The table symbolized the idea that God wanted to have a covenant of fellowship with mankind... and fellowship is best exemplified around a dinner table. Two problems existed, though. First, the Veil of the Temple separated God's presence from the Table of Shewbread. God and man were separated from fellowship because of sin. Secondly, there were no chairs inside the tabernacle. The priests were not allowed to sit down while "on duty" inside the tabernacle. All of their ministry was done while standing. (Ye that *stand* in the house of the LORD, in the courts of the house of our God - Psalm 135:2).

Along came Jesus Christ, God's Son. In His final week of ministry upon this earth, you will remember He partook of one final meal with His disciples (Twelve of them to be exact). This "Last Supper" was actually a fulfillment of what the Table of Shewbread foretold for centuries... God SAT DOWN with man around a dinner table and fellowshipped around a meal... a meal which included bread for 12 men. As Jesus broke the bread He said "This bread is My body, broken for you." You know the rest of the story, right? Jesus went on to die upon a cross for our sins, and, at His death, the veil of the temple was torn in two from top to bottom, signifying that it was done by God. God tore the veil that separated the Table of Shewbread from the Holy of Holies where His presence dwelt. Yes, God's presence was no longer confined to the Holy of Holies... He was now available to sit down at the table with mankind and fellowship with them.

Lest you think that this is all just "coincidental," I will mention a well-known verse from Revelation 3. "Behold, I stand at the door and knock; if anyone hears My voice and opens the door, I will come in to him and will dine with him, and he with Me" (Revelation 3:20). So, you see, Jesus didn't just die so YOU could go to Heaven... He died so that HE could fellowship with you... around the dinner table.

THE BRAZEN LAVER
March 7 | September 4

When a person entered the Old Testament tabernacle the first thing they would see on the way to the Holy Place (where God's presence dwelt) was the ALTAR OF SACRIFICE. The second thing they'd see, and pass by on the way to God's presence, was the BRAZEN LAVER. This is where priests would cleanse themselves with water before entering the Holy Place. So, there was a pattern established. For a person to get into God's presence: 1) a sacrifice must be made, and 2) a cleansing must take place.

This still holds true for all of us under the New Testament... a sacrifice must be made and then a cleansing take place. But, Jesus became the sacrifice upon the Altar of Sacrifice (if you will) so that no more sacrifices for sin need to be made. Now, all that needs to be done for those who have accepted Jesus' sacrifice is to be cleansed in the Brazen Laver (symbolically).

This is where we often get off track.
1. Many think "I've got to get clean before I come to God." No, the FIRST thing you must do is accept the sacrifice that was made for you through Jesus' death. The Altar of Sacrifice comes BEFORE the Brazen Laver.
2. Once you've received what was done for you on the Altar of Sacrifice, God will move you toward the Brazen Laver where you can be cleansed and made Holy for His presence. Cleansing comes AFTER receiving the sacrifice, not BEFORE. (You don't have to "clean your life up" before you accept Jesus... if that were the case the Brazen Laver would have come before the Altar of Sacrifice).
3. If you sin after receiving God's forgiveness through Jesus' sacrifice, you don't have to go BACK to the Altar of Sacrifice. Jesus' sacrifice for sin covers "once and for all" (Hebrews 10:10). All that needs to be done is to go to the Brazen Laver to receive cleansing, so that you can once again enter God's HOLY presence without shame or guilt.

This is why 1 John 1:9 says "If we confess our sins He is faithful and just to forgive us of all our sins and to CLEANSE us from all unrighteousness."

Christ cannot, and will not, be sacrificed again for your sins or mine. When we mess up and sin we don't have to get "saved" again and again. We simply go back to the Brazen Laver for a cleansing. If you've sinned since becoming a Christian, don't beat yourself up about it... just get cleansed! And the way you do that is by CONFESSING your sins.

PRO-VISION
March 8 | September 5

Have you ever gone on an all-day hike before? If so, you probably packed a lunch to take along with you. Why did you do that? You did it because you were "looking ahead" and could see that somewhere along your journey you'd need nourishment and sustenance… so you carried PROVISIONS with you.

The word PROVISION (or PROVISIONS) is found many places in the Bible, especially in conjunction with the word JOURNEY. The word PROVISION is made up of the prefix *pro* (meaning "for") and *vision* (meaning "to see"). So the thought behind the word PROVISION is that you are going somewhere on a journey, in a particular direction, and can "see ahead" that you will need something "for" the journey. PRO-VISION is required.

This leads me to the thought for today. Why does God tell us that He is our PROVIDER? Because He sees the journey we are on, and can "see ahead" that there are things we need "for" the journey. His PROVISION helps us on our journey, so we can get to the place He has called us to go. Just like the children of Israel on their way to the Promised Land… God provided daily manna as PROVISION for their journey.

This is why it's important to never "sit down" or "quit" in the journey you're on. When you stop the journey PROVISION is no longer needed. Very little energy and nourishment is needed for "sitting down." No! Provision is for the journey! Don't sit down and don't quit… PROVISION will continue to come from the Father as you continue to march toward the Promised Land He is calling you to.

MY PRAYER FOR TODAY:
"Lord, I expect Your provision and supply to come to me today as I continue on my journey towards Your will and plan for me. Thank You that You give me everything I need to make my journey a successful one!"

Genesis 22:14 (NLT)
Abraham named the place Yahweh-Yireh (which means "the LORD will provide").

CLOSENESS
March 9 | September 6

My dog, Archie, was especially excited to see me when he woke up one morning. Almost every morning he will come to me and greet me when he wakes up, but this particular morning was different for some reason. He propped his legs up on my lap and buried his head under my armpit. He was wriggling around, excitedly burrowing as much of his upper body into my chest as he possibly could. The best way to describe his behavior is that he wanted to "get inside me." It wasn't enough to be "with me" or "near me." He seemed to want something more than that. Yes, I really think he wanted to get "inside me." What an awesome picture of real love in action!

Archie's actions made me think about David, in the Bible. The scriptures say that David was "a man after God's own heart" (1 Samuel 13:14). He didn't just want to be close to God, or in the same room with Him. No, he wanted to be "inside" God… right next to His heart where he could hear the heartbeat of His Maker.

"Closeness" is a relative term. You can be in the same building with another person and say "We are close." To be in the very same room makes you closer still. To stand right next to the person might make you say "We're as close as you can get." But, there is still another level of "closeness" that can be achieved… and it's based on something more than your location.

When you get "inside the heart" of another person, know their likes and dislikes, know their attributes and character, and are willing to sacrifice your own identity, and lose yourself inside the other person, that's when love has reached its highest form. Isn't that what Jesus did when He laid aside His Heavenly body to become flesh and blood like us? He discarded His rights to Godhood so He could be close to us… He was "after our hearts." He got so close that a woman was healed by touching the hem of His garment. He got so close that parents put their children in His lap so He could bless them. And in total vulnerability, He got so close that men were able to restrain Him, and beat Him, and whip His back, and hang Him on a rugged cross. This is how close He got to us to show how much He loved us. After His resurrection and ascension, He got closer still as He came to make His home "inside the hearts" of all who will receive Him.

God wants to be close to you… He is "after your heart." The question now is "Are you after His?"

THE "FINISHER" OF OUR FAITH
March 10 | September 7

"Looking unto Jesus, the author and finisher of our faith." Hebrews 12:2

I heard this scripture verse being read and the word "FINISHER" rever berated inside of me when I heard it. Immediately, the meaning and defi nition of the word "FINISH" came with new understanding as it applies to this verse. Three thoughts came to mind about the word FINISH.

The first thought that came to mind was the guys who work in construc tion on the final details of a house… there are framers, roofers, and FIN ISHERS. The finishers do all the final details of the house before a family moves in. Likewise, Jesus is the detail person in your life. He is working on the smallest details making sure that your life is pleasing to God, so you can be a home that the Maker of the Universe will be glad to call His own.

The second thought that came to me about the word "FINISH" is one that we all pay attention to during the Olympics. To "FINISH" entails crossing a FINISH line. Needless to say, no runner ever got a medal at the Olympics without crossing a FINISH line. The FINISH line is where re wards are given for endurance, stamina and consistency. It doesn't matter if you were the first one out of the starting blocks… or the last one, for that matter. What matters is how you FINISH! Don't complain about the way you were raised, the surroundings you were brought up in, or the disadvantages you suffered through at the starting block. Don't let that hinder your race! The FINISH line is where you'll get your reward… and Jesus is the FINISHER… if He's *with* you and *in* you, you will succeed!!!

The final thought that came to me about the word FINISH was this: "How important is it to be a FINISHER in life?" The answer comes from the fina words of Jesus upon the cross: "It is FINISHED!" You are here for a pur pose… your life has meaning… it has a beginning and, somewhere down the road, it has an end. At the end of your life, do you want to be able to say with Jesus "It is finished" or will you be wondering if you did everything you were supposed to do? Seek God for the direction of your life today Ask Him what His plan for you is. His plans are not ambiguous. There is finality when a plan has been completely fulfilled. There is satisfaction that the desired outcome was achieved. One day, I want to hear God say to me, "Well done, thou good and faithful servant… *you finished well* !"

GOD IS LOVE... BUT LOVE IS NOT GOD

March 11 | September 8

1 John 4:8 (NAS)
The one who does not love does not know God, for GOD IS LOVE.

Now, even though the verse above tells us that GOD IS LOVE, we cannot flip the words around to say, "LOVE IS GOD."

GOD Himself is so completely saturated in holy, divine LOVE that His name is synonymous with LOVE. He is known for His love. "For God SO LOVED the world that He gave His only begotten Son!" (John 3:16).

Our human LOVE is not the same as God's love. Our love can be directed toward another human, toward an animal, toward a possession or toward any number of things. Our love is not always holy or pure. As a matter of fact, the Bible tells us there are some things that we SHOULD NOT LOVE. For instance, 1 John 2:15 says "DO NOT LOVE the world or anything in the world. If anyone loves the world, love for the Father is not in them." Proverbs 20:13 says, "DO NOT LOVE sleep, or you will become poor; Open your eyes, and you will be satisfied with food." And, most of us have heard the familiar passage in 1 Timothy 6:10, "The LOVE of money is the root of all evil." The Bible is very plain on this issue... it is possible to LOVE someone or something that you shouldn't love. It's also possible to LOVE something that is downright evil. So, just because you LOVE someone or something, that does not mean you are doing "the right thing." LOVE is a wonderful feeling and expression to experience... but it is not GOD.

This world tells us, "As long as you LOVE somebody that is all that is important... Love can do no wrong." That goes under the wrong assumption that LOVE is GOD, and must be obeyed at all costs. What if a man loves another man's wife? Should he obey LOVE at all costs even though the Bible specifically tells him that he is looking at the possibility of committing adultery? No, that man must deny himself that thing or person that he "loves" in order to obey God.

It is always appropriate to OBEY GOD... it is not always appropriate to OBEY LOVE. Yes, God is Love... but remember, Love is not God.

HE CAME TO OUR DARK WORLD
March 12 | September 9

I spent about six hours in the crawl space of my house on a hot summer afternoon, trying to fix a plumbing problem. Now, try to imagine a 6'3" tall man in a space that's only 22" high! Yes, I spent all those hours on my hands and knees… and back… and, sometimes belly. I was crawling over gravel, dirt and mud… and a little bit of sewage. It was dark, dank and stinky, with spider webs and assorted crawling insects adding to my almost intolerable set of circumstances. I was not "made" for that kind of environment. I'm accustomed to being able to move freely, without restrictions and confinement, but that was not the case as I took care of those plumbing issues that day. Needless to say, I was a little sore when my work was done, after bending and contorting in so many uncomfortable positions in those tight spaces.

After my ordeal I had a greater reverence and appreciation for what Jesus did when He left the splendor of Heaven to come to our dark world to fix our problems for us:

- The Omnipresent One, who could be in every place at once, was confined to a single location, inside a human body.

- The One who lives "outside of time" was bound by seconds, minutes and hours as He walked this earth.

- The One who is Omnipotent (All-Powerful) grew tired and fatigued due to His mortal limitations. (On one occasion He was so tired that He slept through a storm at sea in the bow of a boat, and only awakened because the disciples called on Him).

- The One who is said to live in "unapproachable light" was shrouded in darkness as He hung upon the cross.

- And, the One who was completely pure and holy, through and through, carried the ugly stench of our sins upon Himself as He died in our place upon the cross.

Confinement, restrictions, limitations… those were the things that Jesus experienced in His mortal body, even before the mortal pain on the cross. All these things were sacrifices He made for us so He could empathize with us, and redeem us. He who was "of Heaven" came to Earth, so that we who are "of Earth" could go to Heaven. Give Him thanks today.

DARKNESS: A TEMPORARY ILLUSION
March 13 | September 10

On one of my morning walks I stood and watched as beams of morning sunlight pierced through a dark thicket of trees. I reflected on the great power that is contained in light, and also, the great oppression that darkness can bring. It was as if God had whispered in my ear as I heard these words inside myself: "Darkness is only a temporary illusion." With those words resonating within me, I was motivated to ask a question on Google… "What time of day do most suicides occur?" The answer was exactly what I expected… AFTER THE MIDNIGHT HOUR.

I've been sick in the daytime and in the night time, and I'm here to tell you, I'd much rather be sick in the daytime than at night. Darkness can bring a sense of hopelessness and despair. But, remember, darkness is only a temporary illusion. It will not last… there's a light on the other side of darkness. Every morning God reminds us of His faithfulness as the morning sun rises. He reminds us in His word that His very first act of Creation was "Let there be LIGHT!" Light brings hope and healing. Light will come soon enough, so don't despair about the darkness you're experiencing at the moment.

Now, scientists tells us that there will come a day (in the very distant future) when the sun will no longer shine. Eventually that giant ball of fire will "burn out." But that doesn't mean LIGHT will cease to exist! Revelation 22 (the very last chapter in the Bible) comforts us with these words: "There will be no more night. They will not need the light of a lamp or the light of the sun, for the Lord God will give them light. And they will reign for ever and ever" (Revelation 22:5). So, you see, the truth of what was spoken in my spirit is verified… *Darkness is only a temporary illusion!*

FORWARDS OR BACKWARDS?

The Lord himself goes BEFORE you - Deuteronomy 31:8 (NIV)
"Get thee BEHIND me Satan" - Luke 4:8 (KJV)

If you're looking FORWARD you're looking in God's Direction… if you're looking BACKWARD you're looking in Satan's Direction.

CONTEMPORARY?
March 14 | September 11

The word CONTEMPORARY means "belonging to or occurring in the present." Our society encourages us to be "contemporary" in our thinking and beliefs by staying in-sync with the current culture. In so doing, we are put into a position where we must abandon older ideas and principles that we have adhered to and lived by our whole life. These older beliefs, truths and standards have guided mankind for centuries... they are "tried and true."

To me, there's a very important problem that we overlook when we try to live by CONTEMPORARY beliefs and standards. The word CONTEMPORARY contains the word TEMPORARY. The word itself lets us know that these ideas, beliefs and opinions are not long-lasting or enduring. Modern man lives by a current set of principles that are TEMPORARY. Be careful that you don't fall into the trap of trying to be CONTEMPORARY by abandoning age-old truths that have survived for centuries!

Let me illustrate it this way. Let's say that you're sick with a very common ailment that has been treated by physicians for decades using a medication that has a 100% success rate. The medication is available at any local pharmacy. But, you hear of a new drug on the market that also treats the same ailment, with supposedly quicker results. Do you purchase the new drug that has not been time-tested and quite possibly has questionable side-effects, or do you choose the drug that has been used for decades with a 100% success rate? I don't know about you, but I like a "sure thing," so I'll stick with the medication that has a history of good results and no questionable side effects. The same holds true for my belief in the truths found in the Bible, which have had success for centuries. I stick with them, because they're time-tested... CONTEMPORARY beliefs are not.

Listen. You have every right to disagree with, and even openly rebel against, any new ideas coming down the pike that encourage you to abandon long-held beliefs (specifically those found in the Bible). Here's my opinion: any new ideas about morality and "what is right and wrong" must be time-tested before I will even begin to entertain the idea that it might actually be true and correct. If you are a Bible-believing person, hold on to the truths in God's Word. Any new "truths" that are contrary may be CONTEMPORARY but they are also, most likely, TEMPORARY.

OUT OF GOD'S HANDS
March 15 | September 12

I've discovered there are some issues of life where, if you handle them yourself, you take away God's prerogative to do them for you. For instance, most of us have heard the saying "Vengeance is mine, I will repay, says the Lord," so we are exhorted by Paul, "Do not take revenge, my dear friends, but leave room for God's wrath" (Romans 12:19). So, ultimately, if we take our own revenge, we give no place for God to take revenge on our behalf. That area of our life has been taken "OUT OF GOD'S HANDS."

There are other areas of life that we might inadvertently do this same thing. Another example is when we want to be recognized, praised or held in high esteem. Do you realize God wants you to be "lifted up" and exalted, but if you do it yourself, you take away His prerogative to do it for you. That's why James 4:10 says "Humble yourselves in the presence of the Lord, and He will exalt you." Yes, God wants to exalt you, but Jesus reminds us in Luke 14:11 that "Everyone who exalts HIMSELF will be humbled." So, if you want to be exalted, and you do it yourself (instead of letting God do it for you) another area of your life has been taken "OUT OF GOD'S HANDS."

There are many other issues similar to these two that the Bible warns us about, but I will only share one more, and this is a BIG ONE. 1 Peter 5:7 tells us that we should constantly be "Casting all our care upon him; for he careth for you." Do you realize that God wants to carry your cares? But, if you carry them yourself, by worrying and fretting over everything in your life, you have effectively taken your cares OUT OF GOD'S HANDS. He's not going to carry your cares if you're always taking them from Him.

MY PRAYER FOR TODAY:
"Father, help me to trust You by putting my life completely in Your hands. Help me to release all of the cares and worries that I hold on to. I know when I'm worrying and fretting that I'm taking my cares upon myself and taking them out of Your hands. Forgive me."

Psalm 55:22 (NAS)
Cast your burden upon the LORD and He will sustain you; He will never allow the righteous to be shaken.

REPRESENT
March 16 | September 13

A truck pulled out of a restaurant into the median on Highway 31 abou
50 yards from me as I was approaching a traffic light. They were wanting to merge into my lane of traffic. For only a second I thought abou
continuing on without letting the vehicle into the flow of traffic. But
I repented of my selfishness and decided to let the person in. As they
pulled in ahead of me they gave the obligatory hand wave of appreciation. As I pulled in closer to that truck at the red light, I noticed tha
they had a Michigan license plate. When we got to the next set of traffi
lights I noticed that they were headed back toward the interstate. They
had most likely taken a brief stop in their journey to or from Michigan tc
eat lunch in Decatur. The thought occurred to me that the brief momen
of interaction I had with that traveller from Michigan might have beer
their only reference to the friendliness, and/or rudeness, of the people
of Decatur, Alabama. A voice within me said "You are a representative."

Whether you realize it or not, everywhere you go you're being a representative of one thing or another. You represent your family, you represent your city, you represent your business, you represent your race, you
represent your region, you represent your nation, and most importantly
you represent your God. It's an inescapable fact.

People will make judgements about your family, city, business, race, region and nation, many times just through their interaction with you. Ir
the briefest moment of time a decision will be made today about you anc
the people you are associated with, simply because of the way you act
or talk in public. Don't take even the smallest gestures of kindness anc
service towards others for granted! You could very well change a long-
held prejudice or stereotype that someone has wrongly held, just by thei
interaction with you. Be an influence for good.

REPRESENT!

1 Peter 2:9 (NLT)
But you are not like that, for you are a chosen people. You are roya
priests, a holy nation, God's very own possession. As a result, you car
show others the goodness of God, for he called you out of the darknes
into his wonderful light.

GREATER THAN WE DESERVE
March 17 | September 14

A 15-year-old young man helped me prepare for a yard sale that I had at my house. After he had been helping me for over an hour, the thought occurred to me that we had never discussed his wages. So, I asked the boy, "How much do I need to pay you per hour?" With wisdom beyond his years, his answer both impressed me and amused me…. "However much you're willing to pay me."

Maybe you didn't catch the significance of his reply, and maybe he didn't even mean to say it the way it came out, but here are the things I heard in his simple reply:

1. You may value my work and effort more than I value it. I'll let you decide.
2. You may be more generous than what my limited abilities are worth.
3. If I set my own price then I may undercut myself.

The more I thought about his reply, the more impressed I was with this simple wisdom. His response is similar to the one we all should have towards God. Many times I've heard people say things like, "I only want what I deserve," and "I just want to be treated fairly." Do you know that God doesn't give us what we deserve? He gives us so much greater and better than what we deserve. If you were to tell God "Just give me what I'm deserving of" you'd be undercutting His generosity and abundance. Doesn't the Bible tell us that He is "able to do exceeding abundantly above all that we ask or think"? (Ephesians 3:20) Why would we want only the little that we in our limited understanding can think up or ask for, when He can bless us far more abundantly than that?!

God values you more than you value yourself… I can guarantee it… and I can prove it, too. He paid the greatest price, the price of His only begotten Son's life, to ransom you. Trust His abundance in your life, and don't settle for less than what His generosity towards you can afford.

Luke 12:7 (NLT)
And the very hairs on your head are all numbered. So don't be afraid; you are more valuable to God than a whole flock of sparrows.

FAITHFUL IN LITTLE
March 18 | September 15

My friend Clint Lee shared a testimony with me that really blessed and encouraged me. I'd like to share his testimony with you.

Several years ago, Clint got a vision for doing a bus ministry to an underprivileged area of the town he was working in. In his enthusiasm, he knocked on doors and handed out flyers, inviting hundreds of people in that area to the children's ministry at his church. The response? Not as he had hoped or anticipated... two children were all that he picked up the first week of his bus ministry. The second week? The same two kids. The third week? Again, the same two children. As he told the story I was waiting for him to tell me how the number increased by leaps and bounds one magical moment in time. But that's not how the story went. You see, for two years he was faithful to continue that bus ministry... and for two years he brought those same two children to church, faithfully, every Sunday morning.

So, here's a question for you: What do you do when the vision you have doesn't get the impressive results you anticipated? Do you quit? Do you say, "I must not have 'heard God' correctly on that one"? I'll ask another question. Are two children's lives, that are hanging in an eternal balance, worth two years of ministry and service to you?

I may be wrong, but I think God is pleased with, and impressed by, the person who is faithful to do what He called them to do, regardless of the results. God is not looking for big results out of us as much as He is looking for our faithfulness to do the thing He called us to do.

MY PRAYER FOR TODAY:
"Father, I know that many times in my life You have tested me, to see if I will do what You've called me to do no matter how big or small the task might be. Forgive me for not seeing that it was my faithfulness to Your call that You were looking for... not impressive numbers and results. Help me to be faithful... even in the small things."

Luke 19:17 (NAS)
And He said to him, 'Well done, good servant! Because you were faithful in very little, you shall have authority over ten cities.

DON'T GIVE UP
March 19 | September 16

Have you ever said, "I just feel like giving up"? I heard someone say that phrase recently, and out of curiosity I asked, "Just exactly what would that look like for you to 'give up'?" I knew they weren't suicidal, so they weren't talking about ending their life. I've heard people say that phrase many times throughout my life, but never stopped to consider exactly what was meant by those words.

I found the answer to my own question recently while reading Luke chapter 18 in the Bible. In Luke 18 Jesus taught a parable about prayer, and in verse 1 it explains why he told the parable: "Then Jesus told his disciples a parable to show them that they should ALWAYS PRAY and not GIVE UP." Yes, that's what it means to GIVE UP... it means to STOP PRAYING. You see, when you STOP PRAYING you've stopped trusting in God, you've stopped hoping for a favorable outcome, you've stopped fighting the "good fight of faith," you've stopped doing the one thing that can bring change to hopeless situations....... you've GIVEN UP.

So, whatever you do today, don't GIVE UP! Keep on praying, even if it seems your prayers aren't "getting through." Prayer changes things... but only if you DON'T QUIT.

"Never stop praying." - 1 Thessalonians 5:17 (NLT)

WHAT IS WORRY?

What is WORRY? It's a prayer that never leaves your lips. It's an unreleased prayer that grows and festers inside your soul. If you would release it to God you would find relief, but as you continue to meditate on it within yourself the weight of it becomes more than you can handle. The prayer that should have been lifted to God is rehearsed over and over again... to yourself... as if you are God... as if you are the one who can make a difference in the situation. Yes, WORRY is simply a prayer that has been aimed in the wrong direction. It should have been directed to God... instead it's directed to yourself.

Philippians 4:6 (NLT)
Don't worry about anything; instead, pray about everything.

THE MOST IMPORTANT POWER WORD
March 20 | September 17

I was having a difficult time trying to get my dog, Archie, to wake up for our morning walk one day. I went to get his leash and the sound of his dog tag jingling made him open his eyes, but he just continued to lay there on the floor. He didn't budge. I said, "Archie, do you want to go for a walk?" No response. "Let's go for a walk!" I said with a peppy tone in my voice. He didn't even flinch. Getting a little irritated with him, I used a harsher voice, "Come on, Archie, let's go." Still nothing. So, when all else failed, I decided to use the one word that always gets his attention. In the smallest whisper, I said the word… "Squirrel." His head popped up immediately. He stood to his feet and headed for the back door. He was ready to go!

SQUIRREL is Archie's "power word." It's a word that always captures his attention. It's a word that motivates him. Just like Archie, we humans respond to certain words with greater intensity than others. Just type the phrase "power words" into the Google search bar on your computer and you will find hundreds of words that experts tell us have "power" to motivate individuals. Marketing companies take advantage of these words when describing products for sale so they can get the consumer's attention and motivate them to spend their hard-earned money.

This leads me to my thought for today. There is one power word that the Bible tells us captures God's attention more than any other. There is a word that, when spoken from the lips of a believer, always initiates a response from God. It is not a word of manipulation or coercion. It is a word of faith. It is the name JESUS. How much power is in that name "Jesus"? Well, the Bible says that "Every knee will bow to God" at the sound of that name (Philippians 2:10). And Jesus Himself said "Whatever you ask the father in my name it will be done for you" (John 16:23).

The name of Jesus is the most important "power word" there is. Are you using it?

Acts 3:16 (NIV) [Words spoken by Peter after healing a lame man]
"By faith in the name of Jesus, this man whom you see and know was made strong. It is Jesus' name and the faith that comes through him that has completely healed him, as you can all see."

WHAT'S THAT SMELL?
March 21 | September 18

On my way to Huntsville for my Bible Study one night I stopped at a local gas station to fill up my truck with gas. There at the pump I noticed a moist spot on the ground, but since we'd had recent rain I assumed it was only water, so I stepped in it as I pumped my gas. My assumption was wrong… it was gasoline… and I realized it fully when I got in my truck and was trapped inside with the noxious fumes. I rolled my windows down as I drove along the interstate, thinking that the fumes would dissipate. Somewhere along the way I rolled the windows back up and the smell seemed to be gone.

When I got to the Men's Home and sat down to teach I mentioned that I had stepped in gasoline earlier and apologized if there was still a lingering odor. The guys there said, "Man! That's you? We were wondering where that smell came from. It's almost unbearable!" I had gotten used to the smell on my 40 minute trip over and hadn't realized that it was permeating the room I was in. I apologized for the smell, took my shoes off and put them on the front porch of the Men's Home. It's the first time I've ever taught a Bible Study in sock feet!

Now, here's the important lesson in all of this: What we walk through in life can linger with us, without us even knowing it. I've said this before but it bears repetition… our lives bring a fragrance to this world. Just as surely as a rose emits a beautiful fragrance and a garbage truck emits an odious one. We get used to the fragrance we give off and don't realize that it's being either enjoyed or abhorred by others. (You've heard the phrase "stinky attitude" right?)

2 Corinthians 2:14 tells us: "But thanks be to God, who always leads us triumphantly as captives in Christ and through us spreads everywhere the fragrance of the knowledge of Him." The Christian emits a life-giving fragrance to this world. When we walk through tough times sometimes the stench can rub off on us and create an unpleasant aroma. But the one who has Christ inside has an overpowering fragrance that dispels all the toxicity in this world.

So I say this in the kindest way I know how… YOU SMELL! The question is: "Is it a pleasant aroma or an unpleasant one?"

QUIETLY
March 22 | September 19

"Joseph, her fiancé, was a good man and did not want to disgrace he publicly, so he decided to break the engagement quietly." - Matthew 1:1

Why did God choose Joseph to be the earthly father of Jesus Christ? think the above verse has something to do with it. He was a good man who wasn't willing to publicly disgrace Mary when he found out she wa pregnant before their wedding day... so he decided to break the engage ment QUIETLY. Think how rare that is to find a person (either male o female for that matter) who would handle something scandalous such as this in QUIET fashion. These days, if something like this happened, i would have been on the internet, on social media, and everywhere you look... within a matter of minutes.

I don't know what all is included in a person's character for the Bible to call them "good" or "righteous," but I do know that this specific poin is attributed to Joseph being a "good" man... that he didn't "air othe people's dirty laundry" and that he handled private matters QUIETLY (King James version says "privily" which is a version of the modern word "privately"). Can you handle private matters in a quiet fashion? If so you are on your way to being referred to as a "good" person in God's eyes. I not, it's time to make some adjustments!

WHAT IF GOD CAME TO YOU...

What if God came to you and you totally missed Him.
He was standing so close you could have reached out and kissed Him.
And He came as a pauper, not as king or priest,
You expected the greatest, but He came as the least.

Oh, what a terrible shame that would be
If He came to you, but you couldn't even see.
Such was the case when the Great I Am
Came not as a lion but as a gentle lamb.

Sometimes He comes in ways unexpected
And quite often those ways are completely rejected.
So if you want Him to shout, so you'll hear loud and clear
Don't be surprised if He just whispers in your ear.

YOU CAN HEAR HIM
March 23 | September 20

Every day, I walk by the same bamboo-filled hedge row on my morning walk. Every day, the same dog barks at me from the other side of the hedge row, inside his fence. It happens without fail. I've never seen this dog, not one single time, because of the thick cluster of bamboo and bushes that separates us. I don't know if he's a relatively big dog or a small dog. I don't know if he's a black dog, a brown dog or a white dog. I don't even really know that it's a "he"…very well could be a "she." But, one thing is certain… I know that dog exists. It lets me know EVERY DAY of its existence.

Some people have difficulty believing in God because they can't SEE Him. John tells us this fact, "No man has seen God at any time" (John 1:18) and God Himself reminds us that "No man can see me and live" (Exodus 33:20). But, just because we can't SEE Him doesn't mean we can't HEAR Him! You can hear Him speak as you open the pages of the Bible. You can hear Him as you listen to the breeze blow through the trees on a Summer morning. You can hear Him in the mighty roar of the ocean. You can hear His testimony in the birds that sing. You can hear Him in the sound of children's laughter. You can hear His voice in the encouragement given by a friend. You can hear Him when you lift praise to His name and He responds with peace and joy inside your heart. You can hear Him when a man of God speaks His words from behind the pulpit in a Sunday morning church service.

Yes, it is true that God cannot be seen... but He CAN be HEARD. Listen closely and you will hear Him all around you.

"Faith comes from HEARING…." Romans 10:17 (NAS)
"We walk by faith not by sight." 2 Corinthians 5:7 (NAS)

ARE YOU FOOLISH OR WISE?

Want to know whether God considers you a wise or foolish person? Proverbs 29:11 gives us something to think about: "FOOLS vent their anger, but the WISE quietly hold it back." If this scripture verse was the only litmus test for whether you would be considered a fool or a wise person, which category would you fall under?

WHO AND WHAT DOES GOD REWARD?
March 24 | September 21

I searched the scriptures to find out WHO and WHAT God rewards. Here is a short list of the things I found.

1. Those Who Sow Righteousness
The one who sows righteousness reaps a sure reward. - Proverbs 11:18 (NIV)

2. Those Who are Persecuted for Christ's Sake
Blessed are you when people insult you, persecute you, and falsely say all kinds of evil against you because of Me. Rejoice and celebrate, because great is your reward in heaven. - Matthew 5 11-12 (NIV)

3. Good Works
And, behold, I come quickly; and My reward is with Me, to give every man according as his work shall be. - Revelation 22:12 (KJV)

If any man's work abide which he hath built thereupon, he shall receive a reward. - 1 Corinthians 3:14 (KJV)

4. Preaching the Gospel
If I preach voluntarily, I have a reward; if not voluntarily, I am simply discharging the trust committed to me. - 1 Corinthians 9:17 (NIV)

5. Diligent Seekers of God
He that cometh to God must believe that He is, and that He is a rewarder of them that diligently seek him. - Hebrews 11:6 (KJV)

6. Those Who Have Children
Lo, children are an heritage of the LORD: and the fruit of the womb is his reward. - Psalm 127:3 (KJV)

7. Those Who Keep God's Commands
Moreover by them is thy servant warned: and in keeping of them there is great reward. - Psalm 127:3 (KJV)

8. Those Who Show Kindness to Their Enemies
If thine enemy be hungry, give him bread to eat; and if he be thirsty, give him water to drink: For thou shalt heap coals of fire upon his head, and the LORD shall reward thee. - Proverbs 25:21-22 (KJV)

FIGHTING NEGATIVITY
March 25 | September 22

I'm struggling, I admit it. It gets harder and harder every day to stay positive in this world full of negativity. I hear the serpent whispering in my ear, tempting me to partake of the forbidden fruit of criticism, negativity and hatred. It's not the least bit appealing, as the stench of its rottenness on the limb repels me away. Yet, I see so many who've grown accustomed to the stench and draw closer and closer to the tree, not even bothered by its ugliness or its repulsive odor. I wonder… is there something I'm missing? Why do so many continue to pick fruit from this tree that God told us to steer clear of? Even as I sit here and write of how much I loathe the tree perhaps I'm falling into its trap, as I criticize those who so freely partake of it. So, yes, I struggle. To speak of the ugliness of the tree only pollutes my vocabulary and steals from the beauty of the Tree of Life that I once focused upon.

Will it go away if I ignore it? No, this tree is here to stay as long as this Earth keeps spinning. But I, for one, refuse to aid in perpetuating its growth. I realize I won't be able to chop it down or even prevent others from partaking of it, but one thing is certain… I will not continue to help fertilize it.

Ephesians 4:31 (NIV)
Get rid of all bitterness, rage and anger, outcry and slander, along with every form of malice.

TRUST

The word TRUST is an interesting word. It's kind of like the word OVERCOME. Neither word can be fully measured or understood until the person using it has been tested. You can say, "I'm an OVERCOMER," but saying it doesn't make it so. Only by actually overcoming a difficulty or obstacle can a person truly confess to be an OVERCOMER.

TRUST is the same way. You can say "I TRUST the Lord" but you haven't truly TRUSTED until you've been presented with an opportunity where the option is available to doubt.

So I ask you this question: "Do you TRUST the Lord?" Of course when I ask this question you understand that I'm really asking "Have you had an opportunity to doubt Him, but you were determined not to?" That's when you've REALLY TRUSTED Him.

FIRST LOVE
March 26 | September 23

I had an inspiring dream. In my dream I was taken back to when I was a teenager. I was looking through some old photos in this dream. One of the photos showed a sign that said in great big painted letters "God Loves You." It was as if it was the very first time I had seen those words together! A flood of emotions poured out of me as I stood there weeping. The meaning of those three little words had penetrated my heart and brought joy, peace and hope to me. I awoke. It was 3:42 a.m. As I lay there for a moment reflecting on the dream, I was amazed at the raw emotion that I experienced. The tenderness of a once unpolluted heart… that was what I had experienced.

These days the beauty and tenderness of God's truths have been tainted and polluted in my mind and heart due to all the perversity in this world. But, I cannot blame the world solely. Truly, I have had a part to play in the slow decay of my own passion and purity. Maybe I had that specific dream because I read Revelation 2 the day before, where Jesus told the church at Ephesus, "I have this against you, that you have left your first love." (Revelation 2:4)

I've read and said the words "God Loves You" hundreds of times over the years, perhaps thousands. There was a time when those words were read and/or spoken that it filled my heart with peace and joy. To my own shame I must admit, over the years I've grown accustomed and familiar with those words, to the point where it has become KNOWLEDGE and INFORMATION instead of an EXPERIENCE.

Purpose in your heart today to revisit the passion of your FIRST LOVE… that moment in time when the beauty of God's Love was more than just a fact that you knew in your head… it was something you felt in your heart.

MY PRAYER FOR TODAY:
"Lord, forgive me for leaving my 'first love.' There was a time when the words "God Loves You" meant so much to me. I want that restored in my life. Bring fresh meaning to those old familiar words. I don't want to take Your love for granted. Stir up LOVE FOR YOU inside me. Awaken it. It has been dormant for too long. In Jesus' Name I pray. Amen."

FIND TIME TO PRAY
March 27 | September 24

I was teaching my elementary kids from Matthew 14:22-32… the miraculous account of Jesus walking on the water. After we read the story, I asked the kids in my class, "Why do you think Jesus was able to do such a miraculous thing as walking on the water?" The typical answer you might expect came forth: "Because He was the son of God, and God can do anything!"

Then I re-read verse 23 which says "After he had dismissed them, he went up on a mountainside by himself TO PRAY." I asked the kids, "Do you think that this information about Jesus praying is important to the story? Does God include details in the Bible that are unimportant, or was the fact that Jesus spent time alone in prayer that night a very important detail of the story?" We sometimes read over stuff like that and don't give it any thought, unfortunately.

I then encouraged the kids with the same words I leave you with today. When you know an important event in your life is coming up, don't just assume that everything is going to work out just because you're one of God's children. No! Do what Jesus did the night before the miraculous "walking on the water" event… SPEND TIME IN PRAYER, ALONE.

If anyone could have been successful in life without needing to pray, it would have been Jesus, God's Son. Yet, we see Him on many occasions finding a solitary place where He could go alone to pray… to seek God's direction and His power for upcoming events. If Jesus felt the need to pray what makes us think we can manage without it?

Mark 1:35 (KJV)
And in the morning, rising up a great while before day, He went out, and departed into a solitary place, and there prayed.

Luke 5:16 (NAS)
But Jesus Himself would often slip away to the wilderness and pray.

Luke 6:12 (KJV)
And it came to pass in those days, that He went out into a mountain to pray, and continued all night in prayer to God.

SUNLIGHT (SONLIGHT) BRINGS BEAUTY
March 28 | September 25

We have a huge magnolia tree in our front yard, and I was admiring the blooms on it one morning. I wanted to take a photo of one of the blooms so I searched around the tree to find the best bloom to snap a photo of. As I circled the base of the tree, I made an interesting discovery. There were no blooms on the north side of the tree, but there were dozens on the south side

My wife has told me before about the importance of southern exposure for plants, but I never fully comprehended what she was saying until that morning. Since that magnolia tree is so large and densely populated with leaves, the northern side of the tree receives very little sunlight. Little sunlight equates to little growth for flowers… and fewer flowers equates to less beauty on the northern side of this tree. Yes, sunlight is needed for growth, but that morning I got a deeper revelation about sunlight… it's needed for beauty!

1 Peter 2:9 (NIV)
That you may declare the praises of him who called you out of darkness into His wonderful light.

Isaiah 61:3 (KJV)
To appoint unto them that mourn in Zion, to give unto them beauty for ashes, the oil of joy for mourning, the garment of praise for the spirit of heaviness; that they might be called trees of righteousness, the planting of the LORD, that He might be glorified.

RARE BEAUTY

I wrote the following poem in honor of a beautiful patch of yellow bitter-weed flowers that grew up from a crack in a concrete sidewalk.

It doesn't matter to me that they call you a weed
What impresses me most is you once were a seed
That fell in a crack but still could succeed
And bring beauty and color to a world that's in need.

I wish there were more in this world just like you
Who don't make excuses about all they've been through
But just bloom and grow, and drink in life's dew
Your beauty is rare, found just in a few.

THE REAL YOU
March 29 | September 26

"In the heat of the moment, that's when 'the real you' comes out." I've often heard people say this, and I've even said it myself. But more recently I've been rethinking this idea. It's not really scriptural, just to be honest.

This saying suggests that no matter how righteously you might live on a consistent basis, the pressure moments in your life is when the person you really are manifests. So, let me illustrate how this works. Let's say you've given yourself consistently to ministry and service to the Lord for the last several months of your life. You've been selfless, loved others, prayed regularly and stayed in close communion with the Lord all the while. Now, perchance, while on an overseas missionary trip, you're hammering a nail as you install a new roof on an indigenous pastor's house. Your hammer misses the nail and you mash your thumb and let out an expletive, much to your surprise and to the surprise of those around you. Was that momentary deviation from your normal behavior a defining moment of who you are and what your character is? Do all the worthwhile achievements and ministry you performed for the last several months get eclipsed by that one moment of weakness you experienced in your flesh? Of course not! That's ridiculous thinking!

The "real you" is the "consistent you" not the "momentary you." It's the person you are on a consistent basis, day in and day out. God doesn't judge your character based on a single "heat-of-the-moment" flaw. Sure, it wasn't right, nor was it acceptable before God. But, it was not a defining moment of who you are as a person, or as a child of God.

The Bible shows us over and over again that the character flaws of great men of God did not disqualify them from being considered righteous before God. David, in an extreme moment of weakness, committed adultery and murder, yet he was called "a man after God's own heart." Abraham initially doubted God's Word when God told him he would have a son through Sarah, yet he is known as "the father of faith."

Your moment of weakness may have been embarrassing. It may have even harmed your reputation. But it wasn't the defining moment of who the "real you" is. Don't judge yourself so harshly when you've made a mistake. Repent and make it right quickly... then move on.

GOD CANNOT BE MOCKED
March 30 | September 27

In the Spring of 2018, I was on one of my morning walks when I heard the distress call of a Killdeer. Killdeer are known to let out a distress call whenever a person, or predator, gets too close to their nest. I looked all around to see if I could find the bird, but it was nowhere to be found, so I walked on. A few seconds later I heard the call again. I glanced upwards to a fencepost, and there it sat… a mockingbird mimicking the distress call of a Killdeer. That mockingbird fooled me! And now I know, even better than before, the reason it's been given the name "mocking" bird. Not only did it mock (mimic) the sound of a Killdeer… it also mocked (teased/fooled) me.

As I thought about that mockingbird, I remembered the verse of scripture in Galatians 6:7, "God cannot be mocked. A man reaps what he sows."

"God cannot be mocked." That word "mocked" has a two-fold meaning. The first meaning suggests that "God cannot be FOOLED into thinking something that is not true." The second meaning suggests that "God cannot be MIMICKED." You can't imitate actions that look like God and sound like God, but really aren't God. A mockingbird can sound like a Killdeer but it will never be a Killdeer.

Listen, you can say you've been planting good seeds and you can mimic the actions of others who are planting good seeds, but if you've actually been planting bad seeds, you'll reap what you've sowed. You might fool others, but you can't fool God. He has set the seasons in order. There is a planting season and a reaping season. You can't plant poison ivy seeds and expect to get grapes from them at harvest time!

What kind of seeds are you planting? You will reap a harvest one day from the seeds you've been planting. It's guaranteed. God won't be mocked! He can't be fooled… and He can't be mimicked!

Matthew 7:16-17 (Berean Study Bible)
By their fruit you will recognize them. Are grapes gathered from thornbushes, or figs from thistles? Likewise, every good tree bears good fruit, but a bad tree bears bad fruit.

DON'T LOSE YOUR FRAGRANCE
March 31 | September 28

My wife clipped a bloom from our magnolia tree and put it on the kitchen counter. When I saw it there on the counter I got up close to take a whiff. Wow! What an awesome fragrance it had!

A few days later, I passed by the bloom on the counter and noticed that it had started turning brown. After walking by I thought to myself: "I wonder if it still smells as good as it did a few days ago." Out of curiosity I turned around and bent over to take another whiff. In my mind I was anticipating sort of a stench since the petals were brown. I was pleasantly surprised, though, as the awesome fragrance from three days ago still permeated its petals.

So, here's my word of exhortation for today:
Just because you're "getting old" doesn't mean you have to lose your fragrance. I also like to say it this way: "You can grow old without growing mold!"

2 Corinthians 4:16 (NAS)
Therefore we do not lose heart, but though our outer man is decaying, yet our inner man is being renewed day by day.

2 Corinthians 2:15 (NLT)
Our lives are a Christ-like fragrance rising up to God.

POSITIVES ADD... NEGATIVES SUBTRACT

I'm amazed by the number of people who don't think their negativity can harm others. Maybe we should think about our words and attitudes as currency, and our positive words are "adding to" and our negative words are "subtracting from" those we're around. Give me total access to your bank account for one week and I guarantee you'll be hoping that I'm a positive person (adding to your account) instead of a negative person (taking away from your account). How come we can understand the economic effects of negatives but not the emotional and spiritual effects?

Proverbs 23:16 (NIV)
My inmost being will rejoice when your lips speak what is right.

EXPERIENCE FREEDOM... COME CLOSER
April 1 | September 29

When I take my dog, Archie, with me on my morning walk I unleash him once we're inside the gated cemetery that we stroll through. Archie loves being able to run and explore with complete freedom. There's one bad thing about his complete freedom, though. Sometimes he gets too far away from me. Distance can create problems. There is safety in staying close. This morning I had to call Archie back to me... he had gotten too far away.

The Master knows those who have strayed away from His Presence. He sees the danger that is awaiting those who test the boundary lines of their freedom. Many do not even realize how far they've drifted from His Presence. So, although He gives us freedom, He will often remind us to "COME" to Him where freedom can be fully enjoyed. How do I know if I've strayed too far away from His Presence? The Bible says "In His Presence is fulness of joy." (Psalm 16:11) When I've strayed from His Presence there is an absence of joy. The further I stray from Him the closer I'm drawn to fear and worry. When joy is absent, and fear and worry are present, I am not free. In His love He calls me back to Himself... where there is true freedom. Listen closely... maybe you can hear the Master calling out to you, "Come closer... you've gotten too far away."

Matthew 11:28 (KJV)
Come unto me, all you that labor and are heavy laden, and I will give you rest.

WHERE IS YOUR TREASURE LOCATED?

"But lay up for yourselves treasures in heaven, where neither moth nor rust destroys and where thieves do not break in and steal." - Matthew 6:20

If I have a joy and peace that is only obtained through earthly means then that joy and peace can be stolen from me. It's happened to me on many occasions. When troubles and problems come into my life, and I lose my peace and joy, it's a telling moment. I've discovered that my peace and joy were established in earthly things, not in heavenly things. If my peace and joy were established in Heaven then it could not be stolen from me. Jesus made that promise. So, what do troubles and problems do for me? They help me discover where my treasure is located.

A STRONG TOWER
April 2 | September 30

"The name of the Lord is a strong tower, the righteous run into it and they are safe." - Proverbs 18:10 (NAS)

As I was contemplating this verse one morning I received a few nuggets of truth that I'd like to share with you.

1. "The NAME"...

This verse doesn't say that "The LORD is a strong tower." No, it says "The NAME of the Lord is a strong tower." How important is the name of the god/God that you serve? Does it matter if you call Him "Allah," "Buddah," "Baal" or "Jehovah"? If you call Him by the wrong name will you be safe? The NAME is important! Why do you think people in this world grimace when you speak the name of JESUS? Because His name is a TOWER OF POWER! Yes, there's POWER in His NAME!

2. "of the LORD"...

This verse doesn't say that "The name of GOD is a strong tower." No, it says "The name of THE LORD." Calling Him God is one thing... calling Him LORD is another! James tells us that demons believe in God, and tremble (James 2:19). Just because you believe in God doesn't mean that you call Him "LORD." When you call Him "LORD" you are submitting yourself to His rule and leadership. When He is your LORD, you are safe!

3. "is a STRONG"...

His name is not just a tower... it's a STRONG tower. When the twin towers collapsed after being attacked on 9/11 we discovered that man-made towers can be toppled. If you want to be "safe" you need to reside within a STRONG tower... one that your enemy can never penetrate or destroy. The Name of the LORD is such a tower!

4. "TOWER"...

The name of the Lord is NOT a strong bunker... it's a strong TOWER. Now think about that for a minute. All the "bad guys" for the past 100 years have built fortified underground bunkers to try and protect themselves... from Hitler to Bin Laden. Evil men hide underground. But, the righteous run to a TOWER that rises above this earth!

ALL USED UP?
April 3 | October 1

I had a can of Edge shaving gel sitting on my bathroom sink. I picked it up to squirt some gel in my hand... the can felt empty. But, there was enough gel in it for another shave so I didn't throw the can away. Each day, for three whole weeks, I picked that can up thinking I would be squirting out the last bit of shaving gel that was left, and each day I was wrong. I could have thrown the can away three weeks earlier, at the first moment I thought it was "all used up." But, because I didn't, I got almost two dozen shaves out of that seemingly empty can.

Isn't it interesting that something can give every appearance of being empty, when it's really not? You know, God packs a lot of life into each one of us. When we're young the world is new and we are "full" of possibilities and potential. As time progresses, we assume that life is slowly emptying out of us up until the day we breathe our last breath.

Friends, we can't think that way. It is contrary to the way that God created us. Each person is packed with purpose and usefulness up until the day he leaves this planet. Our enemy, the devil, whispers in our ear telling us that we're "all used up," but he is lying! When we're self-focused and self-absorbed we can wrongly agree with the devil's assessment of our lives. But, when we're outward reaching and giving of ourselves, purpose and usefulness continues to flow out from us.

I'd like to encourage you from God's Word. Psalm 92:14 speaks of the blessing of the righteous when it says, "Even in old age they will still produce fruit; they will remain vital and green." Producing fruit! That is your purpose here on earth. Now, what trees are best at producing fruit? Older trees that have been around for years... and decades. Friend, you're not "all used up" and almost empty! There's more life and purpose within you than what you know... a can of shaving gel told me so.

Jeremiah 17:7-8 (NAS)
Blessed is the man who trusts in the LORD and whose trust is the LORD
For he will be like a tree planted by the water, that extends its roots by a
stream and will not fear when the heat comes; But its leaves will be green
and it will not be anxious in a year of drought nor cease to yield fruit.

"THE OSPREY FLIES ALONE"
April 4 | October 2

While on a vacation trip to the beach, I got up early so I could stroll along the beach before the crowds started to gather. It was 5:45am. There was not another soul on the beach but me. I enjoyed a moment of solitude as I listened to the crashing waves and watched the colors of the morning sun illuminate the horizon. I glanced upward and noticed a large predator bird flying overhead. It was an osprey. It soared majestically as it scoured the shoreline looking for its morning breakfast. I was impressed by this bird's gracefulness and beauty. It slowly soared down the beach with only an occasional flap of its wings… in a few moments it was gone. Minutes later a flock of sea gulls flew by. They were noisy and erratic. They squabbled with one another and sometimes fought over the food they found on the beach.

I mused about the difference between the two kinds of birds I had seen… the osprey and the sea gull. As is our human custom, I glorified the osprey for its gracefulness and beauty, and unwittingly disdained the noisy sea gulls as I made comparisons between the two birds. Now, I'm not saying God spoke to me, but inside my heart I heard these words, "But the osprey flies alone." Then it hit me. The sea gulls fought and squabbled with one another… they were noisy and almost irritating… but they flew together… they were a family…they were a team.

You know, it's easier to "do life" on your own… to call all your own shots… to answer to no one but yourself. It's a challenge to work with a group of people… there's conflict… there are opportunities for division and dissension. But, the reality of life is that if you don't want to be alone you've got to deal with imperfections in relationships. You've got to learn to overlook other people's faults (just as they overlook yours) and you've got to learn to "give and take" (with more emphasis on "giving" than "taking"). It can be messy and sometimes almost irritating, but it can also be very rewarding!

As much as you might appreciate the gracefulness and majesty of the osprey in flight, just remember this… the osprey flies alone.

Psalm 133:1 (NIV)
How good and pleasant it is when God's people live together in unity!

THE DISHWASHER GOSPEL
April 5 | October 3

When I put plates and utensils in the dishwasher I usually wash them off pretty thoroughly first. My wife, on the other hand, will put a plate in there with all kinds of food stuck on it. The difference between the two of us is that I don't really trust the dishwasher to do its job totally, so I try to help it out. My wife believes the dishwasher will do its job thoroughly and that there's no need to go easy on it... after all, that's why we bought the dishwasher in the first place... to do the cleaning for us.

I've heard people say, "I need to get myself 'cleaned up' before I go to church and get right with God." Unfortunately, they've applied my dishwasher principle to their lives. They think they need to help God out by cleaning their lives up first before coming to Him. The truth is, it also reveals a lack of faith in God's ability to clean up even the worst messes in our lives. He doesn't need our help, and He doesn't need us to get "cleaned up" before we come to Him. Cleaning us up is His "job" and it's something He takes great joy in doing. So, today, I encourage you to bring your "messes" to God, and trust Him to do the clean up work.

I John 1:9 (KJV)
If we confess our sins, he is faithful and just to forgive us our sins, and to cleanse us from all unrighteousness.

"BIG SINS" AND "LITTLE SINS"

Here's a question for contemplation: Are there "big sins" and "little sins?" Are some sins less damnable than others? Is lying or gossiping less of a sin than murder or adultery? Before you answer that question, think back to the very first sin ever committed. The sin that caused man's eternal separation from God. The sin that caused a curse to come upon the earth and upon mankind. What was that terribly evil and wicked sin that caused our dilemma? Was it murder? Was it adultery? No! A man and a woman ATE A PIECE OF FRUIT! That was it! Was that so terrible? Should that have caused all of mankind to plummet into eternal damnation?! Yet, that one single "little" act of disobedience has contributed to all the pain and suffering that is in our world today. So, before you get too comfortable with telling a "little white lie" or spreading a word of gossip, remind yourself that it was not a "big sin" that started this mess we're in... it was a "little sin" (if there really is such a thing as a "little sin.")

BEING QUIET COULD SAVE YOUR LIFE
April 6 | October 4

We had a baby robin that was hopping around in our yard for over a week, following its mother around, learning how to fly and how to hunt for insects. I was concerned about the little critter's safety because it was a very "vocal" bird. It had a very loud, distinct chirp and it was chirping constantly. The reason for my concern? I have a voracious cat named Pepperjack who is known to torture and kill little varmints that hang around our yard. Dozens of squirrels, chipmunks and birds have fallen prey to his attacks.

My worst fears were realized one morning as I looked out the back door and saw the little robin dead on our patio. Poor little thing. Had it learned to keep quiet it would still be alive today. Its constant chirp became a homing device for Pepperjack to find it, and to eventually kill it.

You know, the Bible is full of wisdom concerning how to take control of our mouths. Our mouths get us into more trouble than all of our other vices combined. People who are always being vocal about their emotions, feelings, grievances and problems are kind of like that baby robin. They unwittingly call the enemy in closer and closer to them by constantly amplifying their life's struggles. The words we say and the attitudes we have can actually attract the enemy to us. Negative, complaining and critical words draw the enemy in "for the kill." It's a wise person indeed who has learned to keep their mouth shut even though they have a right to grumble and complain about their life's frustrations. Psalm 46:10 reminds us to "Be still and know that I am God" and Isaiah 30:15 encourages us with the words "In quietness and confidence shall be your strength."

Yes, you might have a legitimate right to complain and voice your disapproval and frustrations, but will the release of those words help you at all? Is it possible that they could actually hurt you as you call the enemy in closer and closer to your side? Do you know that having a quiet trust in God could actually preserve your life?

James 1:19 (NLT)
Understand this, my dear brothers and sisters: You must all be quick to listen, SLOW TO SPEAK, and slow to get angry.

A GENTLE WIND
April 7 | October 5

I was walking by a magnolia tree during my morning walk when I heard the sound of falling leaves smacking against the branches of the tree. There must have been at least 50 large leaves that fell to the ground at the same time. I had assumed that a large bird or squirrel had caused the commotion, but when I took a closer look there wasn't a single critter to be found among the limbs of the tree. I kind of scratched my head and wondered what caused the stir. Just then a gentle breeze blew and another several dozen leaves fell to the ground. It wasn't a furry or winged critter that had caused the commotion... it was just the wind... a gentle wind at that.

Yes, a gentle wind was all it took to cause the dead, dried leaves on the magnolia branches to be released to the ground below. I don't know if dead leaves hanging on to a living branch zaps any strength or nutrients from the tree, but I know it distracts from its beauty. So, a gentle breeze acts as a pruning device for the tree, helping it to shed dead leaves and limbs.

Ah! What a great reminder, testifying to us of the power of the Holy Spirit in our lives. Isn't the Holy Spirit often compared to "wind" throughout the New Testament? Yes, the gentle wind of the Spirit of God is just what we humans need to rid us of the "dead leaves and limbs" that litter our lives... that are hanging on to us from yesterday. You never realize how many "dead" things are clinging to you from the past until the wind of the Holy Spirit blows over you.

MY PRAYER FOR TODAY:
"Holy Spirit, blow over me and dislodge anything that is hanging on to me from the past that needs to be released from my life. There are things that I'm carrying around with me that I'm not even aware of. But You're aware of them. Blow over me! In Jesus' name I pray, Amen."

John 3:8 (NAS)
"The wind blows where it wishes and you hear the sound of it, but do not know where it comes from and where it is going; so is everyone who is born of the Spirit."'

UGLINESS CAN'T BE AVOIDED
April 8 | October 6

During my walk this morning, I saw a beautifully formed rosebud on a rosebush and wanted to take a photo of it. There was just one problem: it was surrounded by dead, brown stems and buds from previous blooms. When I thought I finally found a good angle that eliminated all the dead buds, I took the photo. When I looked at the photo on my phone there were still a few brown, ugly buds that could be seen behind the beautiful bud. My "perfect world" is not as perfect as I'd like it to be. Only for a second did I consider "photoshopping" the photo to remove the dead buds from the otherwise beautiful scene. But, I had to face reality... the photo told the true story of what I saw... beauty in bloom, right next to brown, dead, ugliness.

This is the reality of the world that we live in. Beauty emerges in the midst of competing ugliness, both vying for our attention, but if you focus on the beauty you won't even see the ugly. I can't eliminate the ugly that exists, but I don't have to pay attention to it. Beauty and good will always shine brighter than ugly and evil. You've just got to determine within yourself to focus on what is good, pleasant and beautiful.

Philippians 4:8 (NIV)
Finally, brothers and sisters, whatever is true, whatever is noble, whatever is right, whatever is pure, whatever is lovely, whatever is admirable--if anything is excellent or praiseworthy--think about such things.

DON'T QUIT!

If you decided today to quit everything you're doing, how many people would it affect? A committed and faithful person recognizes that their decisions don't just affect themselves. You are connected to others who are depending on you to remain faithful and consistent, no matter how insignificant you might think you are in the grand scheme of things. Now, make this simple confession of faith: I WILL NOT QUIT!

Galatians 6:9 (NIV)
Let us not become weary in doing good, for at the proper time we will reap a harvest if we DO NOT GIVE UP.

ARE YOU LEAVING A MARK?
April 9 | October 7

I stood at my bathroom sink and was about to brush my teeth when I noticed a worn spot in the bannister right next to me. I thought to myself, "Now how did that get there?" I picked up my toothbrush, put toothpaste on it and began brushing my teeth as I braced my left hand in that exact same worn spot in the bannister. That's how that worn spot got there! For the last 18 years of my life I've done the very same thing, day after day, without even thinking about it. Eighteen years of bracing my left hand against that bannister as I've brushed my teeth, each day leaving a tiny amount of wear in the finish on the wood. It's amazing what one little consistent action over a long period of time can do!

Some people don't have the proper appreciation for consistency and faithfulness in a person. As a matter of fact there are some who think that staying in the same place and doing the same thing for extended period of time is monotonous and boring. I look at things differently, I guess. When I see someone who stays in a marriage, at a job, at a church, or in a friendship relationship over a long period of time, it makes a lasting impression on me, much like my palm has made a lasting impression on the wooden bannister beside my sink. To flit around like a restless butterfly who never stays in one place too long might be the mode of operation for some, but I prefer the company of people who are well-grounded, who are firmly founded upon God's Word, and who have a track record of consistent faithfulness over long periods of time.

If you're a person who can't find "your place" and have trouble being consistent and faithful in work, church or relationships, consider what kind of mark you're leaving behind you…. odds are there is no mark at all. The mark of faithfulness is only seen after years of constant, consistent behavior and actions. Determine today that you want to leave a lasting mark, a positive impression that will remain long after you're gone.'

Proverbs 20:6 (English Standard Version)
Many a man proclaims his own steadfast love, but a faithful man who can find?

I Corinthians 4:2 (KJV)
Moreover it is required in stewards, that a man be found faithful.

"BORN AGAIN" IS A VERB!
April 10 | October 8

These days it seems like most people use the phrase "born again" as an adjective… as a description of a person. But when Jesus first used the phrase, He intended it to be a verb. Getting BORN is an action, not a description.

There are several reasons why being "BORN" again is an excellent choice of words for the Christian's "entrance" into God's kingdom.

1. Before a baby is BORN they are inside their mother's womb. They are surrounded by darkness for nine months. When they are BORN they come into the light. *(Ephesians 5:8 "for you were formerly darkness, but now you are Light in the Lord")*

2. When babies are BORN they enter the world through a narrow passageway. To be BORN again a person must enter God's kingdom through a narrow passageway as well. *(Matthew 7:14 - "And narrow is the way, which leadeth unto life, and few there be that find it.")*

3. We all understand that EVERY CHILD enters this world through the same entrance way (Caesarean section being the only exception.) I know this sounds absurd, but there aren't some children who came into the world through their mother's mouth, or through their mother's ear, or any other part of their mother's body. There is ONLY ONE entrance way (period). Similarly, there is ONLY ONE entrance way into God's kingdom. So many get this confused these days, saying there are many ways to God. Jesus said it this way in John 14:6 *"I am the WAY, the truth and the life. No man comes to the Father but by ME."*

4. When a baby is in its mother's womb it is alive, but it is not breathing… it has no breath. When the child is born it takes a breath of air for the first time and its life on Earth begins. Before a person is BORN again they are alive yet they are without the BREATH of God… His Holy Spirit. The word SPIRIT in the New Testament comes from the Greek word PNEUMA. This is the word from which we get other words like pneumonia and pneumatic. PNEUMA means "breath or wind". When a person gets BORN again they receive God's BREATH… His Spirit. They're dead spirit is brought to life. *(John 20:22 - And when He had said this, He breathed on them and said to them, "Receive the Holy Spirit.")*

SUBMIT MEANS "YIELD"
April 11 | October 9

Almost all of my life I've heard people use the word "submit" in a negative way. Most people think that being submissive makes you a weak individual. I realize that there are people who have misused the word, and perhaps that is the reason for the negativity. For instance, there are overbearing husbands that have used a heavy hand against their wives by reminding them that the scripture says "Wives, SUBMIT yourselves unto your husband" (Ephesians 5:22).

Well, I was thinking about the word SUBMIT one day as I pondered the scripture verse in James which says, "SUBMIT yourselves therefore to God, resist the devil and he will flee from you" (James 4:7). I decided to look up the word SUBMIT in the dictionary. I found out that it means "to YIELD to another person's authority or will."

YIELDING doesn't sound nearly as controversial as SUBMIT. When you're driving up to a busy intersection in your car and you see a YIELD sign you don't freak out and say, "I'm not YIELDING to anybody! I have my rights!" That kind of attitude could cause a crash, and possibly a death! Well, in reality, that YIELD sign could just as easily say SUBMIT on it. When you YIELD to someone else you are SUBMITTING to them. It doesn't weaken who you are as a person. It just shows that you are being smart, that you recognize a potentially dangerous situation and take precautions before merging with the "traffic of life."

Those who SUBMIT to God YIELD to Him. Listen, life can be very dangerous! There is a devil that we must be on the lookout for... an enemy who wants to cause trouble in our lives. The person who does not YIELD or SUBMIT to God is just asking for trouble. They're pulling out into a busy road without looking both ways and they're just moments away from a collision! Let me put it this way: James 4:7 says to SUBMIT to God and RESIST the devil. You can't RESIST THE DEVIL if you're not first YIELDED (SUBMITTED) to God.

SUBMIT. It really isn't a negative word... not at all. As a matter of fact, it might just save your life one day!

Hebrews 12:9 (NIV)
How much more should we submit to the Father of spirits and live!

DO THE MATH
April 12 | October 10

If you like studying the Bible, and if you like math, too, you'll enjoy this.

1. "After that, He appeared to more than FIVE HUNDRED brothers at once." - 1 Corinthians 15:6 (Speaking of Jesus after His resurrection)

2. "And, behold, I send the promise of my Father upon you: but tarry ye in the city of Jerusalem, until ye be endued with power from on high." - Luke 24:49 (Jesus' words to His disciples before His ascension)

3. "In those days Peter stood up among the believers (a group numbering about a HUNDRED AND TWENTY)" - Acts 1:15 (The day of Pentecost)

Now, watch these numbers. There were 500 followers that Jesus appeared to after His resurrection. He told those 500 to wait in Jerusalem for the promised Holy Spirit. On the day of Pentecost, as recorded in Acts 1:15, there were only 120 followers (of the original 500) waiting for the promise.

Now, get your calculator out and divide 120 by 500. You'll get .24, just one (1) short of .25... or 25%. So only 25% of the original 500 were still waiting for the promised Holy Spirit in Acts chapter 1. Why is this number 25 significant? Because 25% is the same as 1/4th... and 1/4th is the same as "1 out of 4." Why is this significant? Because in the parable of the Sower, Jesus said that only one out of four seeds that were sown by the sower landed on "good soil" which produced a crop of 30, 60 and 100 fold.

Now, remember, Jesus explained the parable of the Sower to His disciples and said that the "seed" was the "word of God." Only 1 out of 4 will actually receive the word of God and get a harvest from it. It's a proven fact, and that's what Jesus explained in the parable, and that's the results we find from the "word of God" spoken from Jesus' lips when he told 500 followers to "tarry ye in the city of Jerusalem, until ye be endued with power from on high." Five hundred heard the Word of God... only 120 received the promise from the Word, because only 1/4th were "good soil" that the word fell upon.

MY PRAYER FOR TODAY:
"Lord, I want to be good soil. When you plant the seed of Your Word in me, I want it to produce a harvest. I want to receive Your promises, so help me be a doer of the Word, and not a hearer only."

BODY WORK
April 13 | October 11

We picked up my son's 2000 model Ford truck from the Body Shop. After his little fender bender from a few months earlier it was in pretty rough cosmetic shape, but after a week at the Body Shop it looked like a brand new truck on the outside. After he drove it I asked him, "So, how did it drive?" He said, "Well, it still drives rough like it did before the wreck, but at least it looks good, now." I laughed. I don't know why I thought it would drive any better than it did before the body work was done... body work doesn't affect the engine... you know that, right?

So here's the lesson I learned from this. You can fix up the body, clean it, paint it, polish it, and even put on "new parts" but if you don't fix the engine, things won't run any better than before (and NO, I'm not talking about automobiles right now).

Matthew 23:27 (NAS)
"Woe to you, scribes and Pharisees, hypocrites! For you are like white-washed tombs which on the outside appear beautiful, but inside they are full of dead men's bones and all uncleanness."

MY OPINION IS....

Recently, somebody asked me my opinion on a controversial topic. Now, if they had asked me 10 years ago I would have spoken up immediately, given a 10 minute dissertation on why I believed the way I do, and shot down any contradictory arguments that didn't support my opinion. But that's not how I responded in this case. I simply replied, "I don't have a strong opinion on that subject." To be honest, I did have an opinion on the topic of conversation, but I didn't think it mattered what my opinion was. My opinion isn't going to change anyone's mind. My opinion is not the final authority. All of mankind will not be judged according to my opinions when they stand before God's throne one day. If you really want to know an important viewpoint or opinion on a controversial topic, go to God's Word, or at least ask God in prayer. After all, He's the One that you will stand before one day. He's the only One whose opinion should matter to you.

Proverbs 18:2 (English Standard Version)
A fool takes no pleasure in understanding, but only in expressing his opinion.

LISTEN... AND OBEY
April 14 | October 12

t was a Wednesday night at church and my group of elementary boys were playing basketball just before our Bible study time. I called out to them, "It's time for our Bible study to begin... drop all the basketballs... don't take another shot... it's time to get started." I turned my back for a moment and a basketball bounced off the basketball rim and grazed my head. I turned around and saw the guilty party. A little boy was standing there, smile upon his face, having just disobeyed my orders. I said, "Why didn't you listen to me!" With great honesty (and just a little too much sarcasm) he replied, "I did listen to you... I just didn't do what you said." As much as I disliked his disobedience, his snide answer became a revelation moment for me.

At that moment I recalled the words of Jesus who said "Why do you call me 'LORD' and do not do what I say?" When we call Him by the name "LORD" we are insinuating that He is the ruler of our lives, and that whatever He says goes. Yet, there are many of us who have heard the words of Jesus all our lives and call Him "LORD" yet still make daily decisions to disobey His commands. We've "LISTENED" but we don't do what He says. Jesus responds to this disobedience by saying, "Why do you even call me LORD?"

Jesus told a parable about people who hear His words but don't do them. He likened them to a man who builds his house on sand. You remember the story. The storm came along, and because the man's house was not built on a firm foundation, it got swept away in a flood. It's a very dangerous way to live life... listening to truth but not obeying it. So, remember, it's better to NOT LISTEN AT ALL than to LISTEN AND NOT OBEY.

Matthew 7:24-27 (KJV)
Therefore whosoever heareth these sayings of mine, and doeth them, I will liken him unto a wise man, which built his house upon a rock: And the rain descended, and the floods came, and the winds blew, and beat upon that house; and it fell not: for it was founded upon a rock. And every one that heareth these sayings of mine, and doeth them not, shall be likened unto a foolish man, which built his house upon the sand: And the rain descended, and the floods came, and the winds blew, and beat upon that house; and it fell: and great was the fall of it.

GOD'S TOUCH
April 15 | October 13

I was leading worship for a small group of elementary children a cou
ple of years ago. In the middle of one of my favorite worship choruse
I looked over and saw a little 5 year old girl visibly moved by the musi
as tears were streaming down her face. After the music was over I sa
down beside the little girl to talk to her. I wanted to find out what it wa
that moved her heart so. I asked her, "Did God touch your heart today?
She looked up at me with a very frightened look. Her eyes got big an
her lower lip trembled a little as she said "What?" Her response and ex
pression led me to know that I had used a phrase she had never hear
before. I suppose the thought of God reaching down from Heaven witl
a great big finger probing inside her chest to touch her beating heart wa
what her little mind conceived as I asked my question. I rephrased th
question: "Did you enjoy the music today?" She smiled big and answere
with an enthusiastic "Yes!"

Perhaps the sound of it frightens you, but the thing we are desperatel
needing in our world is for God to touch our hearts with His presence
His touch can soften the hard and angry heart. His touch can bring peac
in the midst of turmoil and strife. His touch can bring unity where there'
friction. His touch can bring tears where there once was a furled brow
And, one tell-tale sign that His touch has been experienced is that ther
is love were there once was hatred. We don't need change in our gov
ernment… we don't need change in our laws… we need change in ou
hearts! And the only way that will happen is if people will yield thei
hearts to GOD'S TOUCH.

A PREPARED PEOPLE

One of my former neighbors passed away. At her funeral, the ministe
said something that really caught my attention. He said, "God has a PRE
PARED place for a PREPARED people." Those words struck a chord in
side me! God doesn't just "throw things together." He doesn't do thing
on a whim. There is premeditated thought and detail that goes into th
things He does for His people. Jesus said "I go to PREPARE a place fo
you." (John 14:2) So, God is PREPARING something for those who ar
His children. The question is "Are we PREPARING ourselves for Him?"

HEARING VOICES?
April 16 | October 14

We usually consider a person to be strange, or possibly mentally ill, if they say, "I keep hearing voices inside my head." But, isn't it true that we all hear voices every day and respond to those voices regularly?

For instance, anger has a voice, and when you listen to it for a prolonged period of time you'll respond to it and do things that you normally wouldn't do. Cain listened to the voice of anger and killed his brother!

Doubt has a voice, and if you let it talk to you, and don't tell it to "shut up" it will rob you of foundational beliefs that have sustained you all your life.

Fear has a voice, and if you listen to it long enough you will run for shelter even when there's no imminent threat. (Proverbs 28:1 - The wicked flee when no one pursues, but the righteous are bold as a lion.)

Depression has a voice. It tells us that all is hopeless and no joy can be found even though plenty of reasons for hope abound in our lives. It's such a liar.

Lest I sound too negative, I'll also remind you that peace has a voice, and if you listen to it you will rest securely and confidently.

Faith also has a voice, and those who continue to listen to it are seemingly unscathed by anything that the world "throws at them." (Faith comes by hearing, and hearing by the word of God - Romans 10:17) Open up a Bible and you will be listening to the voice of faith!

Courage has a voice, and if you listen to it, it will drown out the voice of fear. It is bold and confident. It knows that "If God is for us who can be against us." - Romans 8:31

Truth has a voice, and if you listen to it you will experience true freedom. After all, Jesus said "You shall know the truth and the truth will set you free." - John 8:32

Yes, we're all hearing voices... there's nothing strange about that. What's strange is how often we tend to let the negative voices drown out the voice of God's Word, the Word that gives us PEACE, FAITH, COURAGE AND TRUTH.

ATTAIN, OBTAIN, MAINTAIN, RETAIN
April 17 | October 15

There are four steps to achieving anything you want out of life, work, and relationships.

1. Attain:
To reach for something that one desires.
2. Obtain:
To receive and firmly grasp what one has desired.
3. Maintain:
To do the work it takes to keep the desired objective within one's grasp.
4. Retain:
Continue to have, to keep possession of that which has been achieved.

The first two steps are fun and there's a feeling of accomplishment in getting them done. The second two are more like work so they're not as fun. Because they're not as enjoyable, we usually have difficulty in following through with these two steps. It takes effort and energy to *attain* and *obtain* what we seek in our lives. For some reason, however, we think that once we have what we want, no effort or energy is required to *maintain* and *retain* what we've received. Marriages fall apart for this very reason. People loose their passion in their job for this very reason. So, here's the truth of the matter: You have not reached success by fulfilling the first two steps… you've reached it when you've done all four.

Romans 12:11 (Moffatt Translation)
"Maintain the spiritual glow."

HOLD ON TO HIS PEACE

PEACE. It's the thing that Jesus died to give me. It's the thing that the devil desperately wants to steal from me. It's the thing I surrender when I engage my soul in issues that don't belong to me. If I hold tightly to it, it will sustain me during trouble and turmoil. If I let it go, I will be no different than the man who says he wants peace but has none, because he doesn't know the Prince of Peace. It's not MY PEACE that I possess, it's GOD'S PEACE. I will not LOSE it to WIN an argument.

Matthew 5:9 (KJV)
Blessed are the PEACEmakers, for they shall be called the children of God.

GOD IS CALLING YOU HIGHER
April 18 | October 16

I had started off the Men's Home Bible Study using Luke 6:46 as my main text where Jesus said "Why do you call me Lord, Lord, and do not do what I say?" I guess one of the guys felt a little intimidated by what I was saying, so he explained his belief that even though we might mess up and not always do what Jesus says, He can still be Lord of our lives. I agreed with his statement. But then a boldness came over me that brought a very challenging word to all in the room… including myself. It was so good that I knew it wasn't from me. So I'm going to try and restate what was said in hopes that it will challenge you today:

"I didn't come here tonight to speak to you on the level you're at. I've come to raise you up to a higher level. We all need to be challenged in our lives. If no one ever calls us up to a higher place of living we will stay stuck in the same rut we've always been in. I'm not here to condemn you, or to make you feel bad about yourself. I'm here to call you to a higher place than you've been, so you can see the person you're GOING TO BE, not the person you ARE. Yes, God loves you exactly the way you are, in your current condition. But He has a vision of the person you're becoming. He will not always speak to you on the level of your current condition. He will challenge you with words that will help you become the person He sees that you will be.

He called a man who had no children "a father of many nations" because He saw what Abraham was going to be. He came to Gideon, a man who was hiding in a wine press from the Philistines, and called him "Mighty man of valor", because he didn't see the frightened, timid man that he was, but He saw the warrior that he would be.

God will speak to you on a higher level than you're comfortable with, but it's with the intention that you become the person He's calling you to be… that you not stay the same… that you stop making excuses about why you aren't progressing… that you stop being comfortable with your failures and defeats. If you plan on serving Him He will continually be calling you to a higher level. The question is, Do you want to go to that higher level?"

NOT DEAD, JUST DORMANT
April 19 | October 17

My wife had picked up some sod at a local landscape company. When I saw the dry, brown stacks of sod sitting in the back of my truck I said, "This sod is dead!" My wife replied, "No, it's not dead… it's just dormant." Now, there's a word I hadn't thought about in a while…DORMANT. I looked up the word to verify that I understood the true meaning. The definition goes something like this: "temporarily devoid of external activity but capable of becoming active later on; alive but not actively growing." You know, during the winter months more than half of all we see in nature goes through a dormant state. Trees are alive, but they look dead… they're just inactive FOR A SEASON. Grass is dry, brown and brittle and gives the appearance that it's dead, but it's not… it's just dormant.

Winter is an especially good time of the year to appreciate and understand that there are "seasons" to our lives. Some things may appear to be dead and lifeless in your life but it's just an illusion. You're seeing the dormancy of winter. If you don't give up hope and cave in to depression and sadness you'll remember that Spring is only weeks away. Soon buds will appear on the trees, color will come back to the grass, tiny flowers will bloom and signs of new life will be seen everywhere. Yes, it may appear like winter has killed everything but don't be fooled… new life, fresh hope, and days of promise are ahead. Just a little word of encouragement I received from a stack of brown, dormant sod.

FORCED FREEDOM?

A person can be forcibly bound, but they can't be forcibly freed. God knows this, and the devil knows this. The devil won't ask for your permission to put shackles on you. He does it by force. But, God won't remove shackles from you against your will. He OFFERS freedom but will not force it upon you. Jesus said, "The truth will set you free." Freedom comes when a person hears the truth and makes a decision to accept it and believe it. You were forced into bondage, but freedom is your choice.

John 8:32 (NIV)
Then you will know the truth, and the TRUTH will set you free.

John 14:6 (NIV)
Jesus answered, "I am the way and the TRUTH and the life."

THE VOICE OF GOD
April 20 | October 18

Have you ever heard a Christian say, "I've never heard God speak to me in a personal way." Usually, what they mean by that is they've never heard Him speak with an audible voice. Ask that same person, "Have you ever heard the devil speak to you?" They would probably reply with, "Yes, definitely!" Yet, I know they've not heard the audible voice of Satan himself. When they respond "yes" to the question of hearing the devil's voice, they're usually referring to an inward feeling or "leading" that is guiding them to make wrong choices or to follow lustful desires. They didn't hear an actual voice…they had impressions on the inside of their soul that they knew were wrong to carry out.

So, if we designate those negative "impressions" as being the "voice of Satan" (and rightfully so) should we not also conclude that when we have inward impressions to do good and to be a blessing, that we are hearing and responding to the voice of God?

Why do we think that we must hear an audible voice to know that God is speaking to us? If we realize that we often hear the devil's "voice of temptation" and have come to recognize that voice, surely, since God is so much greater than the devil, God must be speaking to us more regularly and with greater fervency than the enemy of our souls!

Let this thought sink into your soul, for I believe these words came to me to share with you because GOD SPOKE THEM TO ME. You see, these words written on this page were thoughts that came into my heart on one of my morning walks. If you will, I heard the voice of God speaking these words on the inside of me, and I wrote them down to share with you.

YOU CAN HEAR THE VOICE OF GOD. HE IS SPEAKING MORE THAN YOU GIVE HIM CREDIT. Every time you respond to the inward impression to do good and to bless and encourage others, you are responding to THE VOICE OF GOD.

1 Kings 19:11-12 (KJV)
And after the earthquake a fire; but the LORD was not in the fire: and after the fire a STILL SMALL VOICE.

PAINFUL REMINDERS
April 21 | October 19

Revelation 21:1
Then I saw a new heaven and a new earth, for the first heaven and th
first earth had passed away..."

I was watching a movie one night about a man who wanted to move to
new home because of the painful memories he had of his deceased wif
in the home he was living in. When familiar surroundings carry painfu
reminders of the past sometimes you just need new surroundings.

I wonder if that's why God is going to make a new heaven and a nev
earth. This old earth has gathered so many painful reminders of sin, sick
ness, disease, poverty, hatred and war, that God has decided a new eart
with totally new surroundings will help us completely forget all of ou
past failures and heartaches.

Yes, maybe that explains the new earth part of the equation... but wh
the new heaven? After all, heaven is a perfect place and can't be improve
upon. But, thinking back, there was a moment in heaven's history tha
was "less than perfect," when Lucifer led an angelic rebellion against Go
and was banished from heaven. Maybe this moment in heaven's past i
one that God Himself would like no reminders of. Maybe this is why
new heaven will be necessary.

Of course, these are just speculations, and I can't say with certainty God
reasons for a new heaven and new earth. There is one thing that totall
wrecks my "painful reminder" theory, however. The Bible tells us tha
even though we all will receive new, glorified bodies in heaven, Jesu
Himself will still retain the scars from His crucifixion. Talk about pain
ful reminders! Yet, this is one painful reminder of Earth that we all wil
observe throughout eternity as we worship "the Lamb Who was slain
Maybe it is a "painful reminder"... but it is also a glorious reminder o
the great worship that our Savior is worthy of, and will forever be worth
of throughout eternity.

Revelation 5:9 (NIV)
And they sang a new song, saying, "Worthy are You to take the book an
to break its seals; for You were slain, and purchased for God with You
blood men from every tribe and tongue and people and nation.

FOOLED BY A FRAGRANCE
April 22 | October 20

There was a construction site at the end of my street that I walked by every morning on my morning walk for several months. A port-a-potty stood in front of the site. Believe it or not, that port-a-potty actually smelled really good! No joke! They put some kind of air fresheners in it that constantly gave off a really fresh, perfume-like smell. Sometimes when I would walk by it I would actually take an extra whiff as I enjoyed the pleasant aroma. Well, let me tell you, that "pleasant aroma" was a giant, deceptive LIE!

One morning I was passing by that very same port-a-potty while a guy was servicing it. He had a big tank on the back end of his truck and he was "vacuuming out" the contents of the potty. Oh my goodness! As I walked up I was about to engage the service guy in conversation, but then the smell hit me like a ton of bricks. I thought I was going to gag! I held my breath and walked as quickly as I could to get past the stench. That port-a-potty fooled me for months with the perfume-like smell that emanated from it... but after that moment in time, I was no longer fooled!

In Matthew 23:27 Jesus called the Pharisees "whitewashed sepulchers full of dead men's bones." In other words they looked good on the outside but there was nothing but the stench of death on the inside. Listen, people can fool you. They can make you think by all outward appearances that they are "fresh as a daisy" when, in reality, there's a cesspool inside them. The truth will come out one day, sooner or later. One day everyone will stand before God, and even if they've fooled others about the true fragrance of their lives, God will not be fooled.

Yes, the truth is that we all have a fragrance about us. Some seem to have a "stinky" attitude, while others seem to emanate a sweetness and pleasantness that comes from Heaven. But, God's nostrils will be the final determining factor of whether the fragrance we gave off was just a cover-up masking our true identity, or if it was the essence of Christ within us.

2 Corinthians 2:15
For we are to God the sweet aroma of Christ among those who are being saved and those who are perishing.

ZOMBIES
April 23 | October 21

I don't think it's any coincidence that one of the most popular movie genres in our modern culture deals with Zombies. Think about what a zombie is... it's a person who is walking around like they're alive but they're really dead, but they don't know it. To top it off, the zombie's life consists of nothing more than mindlessly searching for human flesh to devour.

God told Adam and Eve that if they partook of the Tree of the Knowledge of Good and Evil that they would "surely die." Now, we know that they didn't drop dead "physically" on the ground the moment they ate... but they DID DIE. And here's where the similarity to zombies occurs. You see, all of mankind (outside of Christ) is dead spiritually. Sure, they're walking around as if they're ALIVE but inside they are DEAD. What's more, these DEAD people are out walking around trying to find FLESH to devour. They have no appetite for spiritual things because they are DEAD spiritually. They mindlessly grope for another FLESH meal because that is the only thing that seems to be available for food and sustenance.

When a person comes to Christ, however, and surrenders their life to Him, they are REBORN. They are made ALIVE spiritually through rebirth. Gone are the days when they only desired FLESH to eat. They discover that there is new LIFE in Christ... there is a spiritual aspect to life that they were not aware of. Jesus said "Blessed are those who hunger and thirst for righteousness, for they shall be filled." Flesh appetite is replaced with spirit appetite.

The more I think about it, the more I can see it plainly. The Zombie Apocalypse is already underway, and the only thing that can rescue us from certain doom is for all the zombies out there to find new life in Christ... that is the only cure!

Galatians 5:15-16 (NIV)
But if you keep on biting and devouring each other, watch out, or you will be consumed by each other. So I say, walk by the Spirit, and you will not gratify the desires of the flesh

BELIEFS, WORDS, AND ACTIONS
April 24 | October 22

It is possible to have a belief that you never speak out loud, or that you never act upon. Therefore, belief is not the same as faith. Faith requires actions.

If you speak out about your belief you are making an outward affirmation about what you believe inwardly. In essence, your "invisible" belief becomes "visible." So, when you speak words that affirm your belief you are taking the first and smallest step of faith. You see, faith involves actions. That's why the book of James says, "Faith without works (actions) is dead" (James 2:17). Until a belief is at least spoken it has not become faith. (Remember that Ephesians 2:8 says that we are "saved by grace through faith." FAITH is essential to the salvation experience.)

Now, here's where it gets interesting. You see, we've all met at least one person in our lifetime who has spoken words about their belief, yet the rest of their life's actions did not line up with their words. So, we called them a hypocrite. Why did we do that? A hypocrite is someone who has a belief that they've spoken (using WORDS) but their other actions are contrary to what they've spoken. So, yes, you can get saved through faith but the Bible tells us over and over again, "The just shall LIVE by faith." Living our lives by faith is the ultimate ACTION that verifies our inward BELIEFS.

So, here's the way it works:
1. BELIEF: A person has a BELIEF inside them that Jesus is the Christ, the son of God (they are not yet saved because no FAITH is involved… no WORDS or ACTIONS have been used. Remember Ephesians 2:8)
2. WORDS: A person speaks out the WORDS of their belief and that is faith in action… they are now saved according to Romans 10:9 "If you confess with your mouth (WORDS) Jesus is Lord and BELIEVE in your heart that God raised Him from the dead, you will be saved."
3. ACTIONS: When a person's ongoing ACTIONS line up with their inward belief that Jesus is their Lord, they are LIVING BY FAITH. All three things line up in their lives… BELIEFS, WORDS, and ACTIONS. They will not be considered a HYPOCRITE… not by people, and most importantly, not by God.

Romans 1:17, Galatians 3:11, Hebrews 10:38, Habakkuk 2:4
The just shall LIVE BY FAITH.

GOD DRIPS WITH GOODNESS
April 25 | October 23

On my walk one morning I was just spending a little time praising God. Without any premeditation or forethought, these words came from my mouth: "Lord, You're so good that you DRIP WITH GOODNESS!" As soon as I said those words I knew that even though they came from my lips, they were really words that God inspired me to say. I was energized by those words, and by that thought.

GOD DRIPS WITH GOODNESS!

He is so completely GOOD that He is saturated with GOODNESS. It overflows from Him. He has no cut-off valve. Those who get near Him can't help but experience His GOODNESS because it drips from Him. Didn't David say "MY CUP RUNNETH OVER"? When we focus on God's GOODNESS our cup is filled to the brim… but that is not enough for God… He is a God who is MORE THAN ENOUGH… He makes our cups overflow.

He can take five loaves of bread and two fish and feed 5,000 people with it, and still have 12 basketfuls of LEFTOVERS after everyone has eaten… because He drips with GOODNESS.

He can tell experienced fishermen who haven't caught a single fish all night "Drop your nets on the right side of the boat" and they catch so many fish that their boat begins to sink… because He drips with GOODNESS.

We have limited-sized containers to hold God's blessings in. He ignores our limitations… because He drips with GOODNESS!

My Confession for Today: I won't settle for "NOT ENOUGH" or for "JUST ENOUGH" because God is "MORE THAN ENOUGH" and He drips with GOODNESS. If He's the One filling my cup it's sure to overflow!

2 Corinthians 9:8 (NAS)
"And God is able to make all grace abound to you, so that always having all sufficiency in everything, you may have an abundance for every good deed."

SHAKE IT OFF!
April 26 | October 24

When Jesus sent out the 12 disciples to preach the kingdom of God He told them what to do if they were faced with rejection… He said, "Shake the dust off your feet when you leave" (Mark 6:11). It's hard to believe that anyone would reject the preaching and sharing of such wonderful news, but it happened back then, and it still happens today. Sometimes when your message is being rejected it feels like YOU (personally) are being rejected.

What do YOU do when you face rejection? Do you throw a pity party? Do you wallow in your defeat? Do you let that moment of dejection define who you are?

Jesus has a word for such occasions… "Shake the dust off your feet when you leave!" There's more to this message than what first meets the eye.

If you've ever played baseball or softball you probably know what it's like to strike out. On the way to the bench you might feel pretty rotten for your failure, but if you had a good coach, more than likely you heard them say these words… "SHAKE IT OFF!" They didn't want you to carry those feelings of dejection with you because it would hinder your performance the rest of the game. That's what you've got to do when you feel rejected and dejected… you've got to SHAKE IT OFF!

But there's another part to what Jesus said. He said, "Shake the dust off your feet WHEN YOU LEAVE." Did you catch that? "When you leave" means that you're moving on… you're going somewhere else… you're not sitting down and wallowing in self-pity. The 12 disciples had other cities to preach the gospel in. If one city rejected their message they weren't to be bothered by it. Their job was to reach out to as many cities as they could, so if one city rejected them they would just move on to another city and give someone else a chance to hear the good news.

If you're struggling with feelings of rejection and dejection, I know exactly how you feel. We've all been there before. But, no good can come from you wallowing in self-pity. There are other people out there who need you, and need to hear your message, but they won't be helped until you SHAKE IT OFF and MOVE ON.

HE WON'T LET GO
April 27 | October 25

When my kids were younger and I was teaching them how to ride thei
bikes I would push them from behind and would tell them to keep pedal
ing. All the while, my hand was stabilizing them, and their bike, as I hel
on to the back of the bike seat. There were many times that they though
they were on their own, doing it by themselves... they didn't know m
hand was still guiding them and holding them up.

I want to give you an important piece of information today: "You ar
not alone." The hand of God is guiding you even though you think you
have everything under control. Even when it seems like He has "let you
go" He's still in control and guiding your situation. He has promised to
"never leave you or forsake you." Yes, an unseen hand is guiding you
keeping you safe and holding you up even when you're not aware of it..
He'll never let go.

Genesis 28:16 (KJV)
"Surely the LORD is in this place; and I knew it not."

PRAYER

It's the most important and powerful thing a person can do.
It changes hopeless situations into hopeful situations.
It connects an earthly person to a heavenly kingdom.
It refuses to let circumstances determine the outcome.
It brings peace where there is confusion and strife.
It gives us access to the provision of God's Hand.
It gives us a glimpse of God's face.
It is a weapon against the enemy of our souls.
It relieves us of worry and fear.
If you have no other options but PRAYER,
you have the greatest option of all!

Colossians 4:2 (NAS)
Devote yourselves to prayer,
keeping alert in it with an attitude of thanksgiving;

1 Thessalonians 5:17 (KJV)
Pray without ceasing.

LIGHT AND DARKNESS
April 28 | October 26

Mark 11:35 (NLT) [Words of Jesus]
"Make sure that the light you think you have is not actually darkness."

There are people who have lived their whole life in spiritual darkness. I guess you could say that "darkness" is the only "light" they have ever known. If you were to ask them to describe "light" you would get a description of darkness. So, when they are finally exposed to the true light it is painful to them, much like light hurts the eyes of one who has been in a dark cave for several hours and suddenly steps into bright sunlight.

If your definition of *light* is formed by your understanding of darkness it's time to learn the correct definition. It is an embarrassing moment when you are faced with the reality that you haven't been defining the word *light* properly. At that moment you have two choices. 1) You can either admit that your definition of *light* has been wrong and change it, or 2) You can deny the facts and continue to believe that your definition is correct. When you choose the second option you become the one of whom Jesus spoke in the scripture verse above: "Make sure that the light you think you have is not actually darkness."

There is a reason why Satan is called "the prince of darkness." There is a reason why Colossians 1:13 calls Satan's kingdom "the kingdom of darkness." There is a reason why Ephesians 5:8 speaks to our previous nature (before being born again) as "For you were once DARKNESS, but now you are light in the Lord."

Light has rescued us from darkness. Those who remain in spiritual darkness do so only because they have not yet seen the light, or, because they've seen it but think that their darkness is light. Believers are called to reach out to the first group of people… the ones who have not seen the light yet. What about the ones who *have* seen it yet reject it? You can try your best to shine the light before them, but you've got to understand that they think their darkness is light… and they think your light is darkness.

Isaiah 5:20 (NAS)
Woe to those who call evil good, and good evil; Who substitute darkness for light and light for darkness.

LOOK NOT TO THE RIGHT OR THE LEFT
April 29 | October 27

On my walk one morning I was spending some time in prayer, and felt myself getting distracted, both physically and mentally. As I walked along, trying to pull myself back into focus, I got a picture in my mind of a horse with blinders on its eyes. The blinders help keep the horse focused on its journey so it won't be distracted by things on either side of the road.

When that picture came into my head so also did a portion of a familiar scripture verse: "Turn not to the right or to the left." When I got home I looked up that scripture verse and came to realize that there was not just ONE verse containing these words, but SEVERAL.

Jesus has called me to walk on a narrow road. There are distractions on the right and on the left (yes, you can take that politically if you want to). If I get too distracted, my eyes are taken off the road I'm on, and it won't be long until I'm "in the ditch!" So, here are some scriptures for today that will hopefully keep us focused on what is really important and prevent us from being distracted in our journey:

Joshua 1:7 (NIV) "Be strong and very courageous. Be careful to obey all the law my servant Moses gave you; do not turn from it TO THE RIGHT OR TO THE LEFT, that you may be successful wherever you go."

Proverbs 4:26-27 (NAS) "Watch the path of your feet and all your ways will be established. Do not turn TO THE RIGHT OR TO THE LEFT; Turn your foot from evil."

Isaiah 30:21 "And thy ears shall hear the word of one admonishing thee behind thy back: This is the way, walk ye in it: and go not aside neither TO THE RIGHT HAND, NOR TO THE LEFT."

Deuteronomy 5:32 (Douay-Rheims Bible) "So you shall observe to do just as the LORD your God has commanded you; you shall not turn aside TO THE RIGHT OR TO THE LEFT."

Deuteronomy 28:14 (NIV) "Do not turn aside from any of the commands I give you today, TO THE RIGHT OR TO THE LEFT."

PUSH THROUGH THE CROWD
April 30 | October 28

When you read through the Gospels you will find that Jesus oftentimes had crowds of people surrounding Him. The crowds were so large that people in need had a difficult time getting to Jesus. I guess you could say that those in need had to PUSH THROUGH THE CROWD to get to Him. Here are three instances where this happened.

1. Luke 5:18-19 - A paralyzed man on a stretcher couldn't get to Jesus because Jesus was in a crowded house filled with scribes and Pharisees… people that Jesus often labeled as "Hypocrites." The truth is, some people won't come to Jesus because "there are too many hypocrites in the church"…an excuse that has been used for centuries. If you want to get to Jesus but you let others get in the way, then you must not want or need Him badly enough. The friends of the paralyzed man climbed to the roof of the house that Jesus was in and tore a hole in the roof to let their friend down so Jesus could heal him. They PUSHED THROUGH hypocrisy!

2. Luke 8:43-48 - The woman with the issue of blood "pressed through the crowd" to touch the hem of Jesus' garment and she received healing. If you need healing, sometimes you've got to press through the hindrances that other people create as they stand in the way between you and the miracle you seek. Are you in need of healing? Don't let anyone or anything hinder you from getting to Jesus. PUSH THROUGH the hindrances.

3. Luke 19:2-4 - Zaccheus couldn't get a glimpse of Jesus because he was a short man and a crowd of people stood between him and the Master. But did that stop him? No! He climbed up in a tree to see Jesus. His short height put him at a disadvantage, but he found another way to see the Master. Zaccheus became a new man that day, because he PUSHED THROUGH his shortcomings.

There have been crowds of people hanging around Jesus since the time of His ministry here on Earth. Don't let other people hinder you from getting to Him. Doubtless, there are people around Him that you won't like, think are hypocrites, or just would rather not be around…but if you want to get to Him you'd better learn how to push through the crowd!

INVOKE A BLESSING
May 1 | October 29

I was leading a Bible study on the Feeding of the 5,000. I asked a young man in the group to read the story aloud for all in the room to hear. He was reading from one of the newer translations of the Bible. When he got to the place where it says that Jesus BLESSED the bread and fish, his translation said He "gave thanks" instead. At first I didn't think much about it, but the next day I decided to look up other accounts of the Feeding of the 5,000 in that same version of the Bible. In both Mark's and Matthew's account the words "He blessed" was substituted with "He gave thanks" (Mark 6:41, Matthew 14:19). Does the difference in the translation change any meaning to this verse? I think it does, and here's why....

The word BLESSED found in Mark 6:41 and Matt. 14:19 is the Greek word *Eulogesen*, from which we get the word *Eulogy* (a speech given at a funeral in which the deceased is SPOKEN WELL OF). As the word is used in these two verses it actually means something even more than "to speak well of." It suggests that the things being blessed are being "consecrated for divine use." Jesus didn't just "give thanks" for the bread and fish in the story. He consecrated them for divine use. He transferred them out of the realm of the natural into the realm of the supernatural so that God could do a miraculous work with them… that's what a BLESSING does!

Now, don't get me wrong. GIVING THANKS is much-needed and totally appropriate. But, there are times when a BLESSING needs to be invoked on the things in our lives so that they can be "consecrated for divine use." When we BLESS the things, the people and the situations in our lives we see the potential that can be achieved if God's power and blessing are added.

The very first BLESSING that we read of in the scriptures is in the beginning when God BLESSED what He created with the words "Be fruitful and MULTIPLY." You see, when Jesus BLESSED the bread and fish He was invoking God's power to MULTIPLY. That's why five loaves of bread and two fish were able to feed so many people… the BLESSING brought MULTIPLICATION.

If it seems like things are DIVIDED and things are being SUBTRACTED from your life it may be time to invoke a BLESSING… Don't just "give thanks" for what you have… invoke a BLESSING (consecrate it for divine use) and then watch it MULTIPLY.

BLESS "THE CURSED"
May 2 | October 30

While speaking on the topic of Blessings and Curses at a Bible Study, I asked a question. "How many of you have felt like your life or your family has been under a curse… like you've had a string of bad luck and nothing ever goes right?" A few of the men raised their hands. One man explained his reason for raising his hand. "All of the men in my family, every single one, are either currently in prison or have been in prison… all except for me and my son." When he said those words I was stirred to action, just as if I was sitting on a beach watching a man drowning in the ocean. I sprang from my chair and quickly walked over to the man, putting my hand on his shoulder. "The curse stops here" I said boldly without any hesitation. Quite frankly I was shocked by my own boldness.

I prayed for the man out loud proclaiming an end to the curse in his family and sparing him and his son from the repercussions of the curse. I guess you could say that I "cursed the curse." But then I did something more as God's Spirit was empowering me with His boldness. I spoke out a blessing over his life and the life of his son. I could tell that just "cursing the curse" was not enough. No, a counterattack needed to be made to reverse the effects of his "family curse." I spoke out words of favor, blessing and prosperity… a new direction for this man and his son. Perhaps during that moment in time that man's destiny was redirected by a simple obedience to speak a blessing to counteract a curse. I don't know. All I know is that the strange unction I had to move to action was both alarming and exhilarating at the same time.

Friends, there are people drowning in an ocean of curses, struggles and hardships. They're all around us. Many times we don't even see it because they don't cry out for help… they drown silently while others pass by and watch. Open up your heart today to see if you might be called in some way to rescue a drowning soul by releasing a simple blessing over someone…throwing them a life preserver with words that will buoy them up and give them hope for their future. Remember, we are called to be "like Christ" and we all know of His life-saving skills.

Psalm 82:4 (NIV)
Rescue the weak and the needy; deliver them from the hand of the wicked.

TAKING THE BLAME
May 3 | October 31

I was blessed and pleased to hear about a person who humbled them
selves in an attempt to mend a rift they had with another person. Espe
cially considering that the person who humbled themselves was reall
not even at fault, yet accepted blame for the tension in the relationship
It takes a lot of guts to make yourself vulnerable like that, even when yo
know you've done nothing wrong. I don't know if the whole issue got re
solved or not, but I do know that the person exemplified Christ-likenes
in what they did. You see, there was once a giant rift between mankin
and God. Man created the rift by his own selfishness, rebellion and sin
Yet, God humbled himself and came down on our level and, in an at
tempt to remedy the situation, took the punishment we deserved so w
could be reunited with Him. That's the goodness and mercy of God.

You may say to yourself, "I'm not apologizing for something I didn't do
I'm not going to accept blame for a problem I didn't create, and I'm defi
nitely not going to take the punishment that the real offender deserves!"
Go ahead… you have a human right to say that. Just know this: if you wan
to really be like God on this earth, somewhere along the line you'll have t
humble yourself if you want your relationships restored. God showed u
the way to do it when He sent His Son to reconcile us to Himself.

PRAY FOR PEACE

I was praying for a woman who had been through a very traumatic expe
rience. I struggled with finding the words to pray. As I tried to imagin
myself in her situation, with the deep pain and sense of loss that she ha
experienced, I could think of nothing that would bring relief. Then, from
deep within me came these words, "I know it may be a long time befor
she experiences JOY again, but Lord, let her experience PEACE at this mo
ment in time." PEACE carries us through times when JOY can't be found

Joy is the pinnacle of all human emotion. But, when tragedy strikes joy i
elusive. That's when God's PEACE does something that JOY cannot do… i
sustains us when we can't find a reason to go on. A calm assurance come
from God that tells us everything will be alright, even though everythin
seems to be in chaos at the moment. PEACE fills the empty place that JOY
once occupied. When JOY is nowhere to be found pray for PEACE.

THE MIDDLE, AND THE OTHER SIDE
May 4 | November 1

On that day, when evening came, He [Jesus] *said to them* [His disciples], *"Let us go over to THE OTHER SIDE. - Mark 4:35*

When we're in THE MIDDLE of our circumstances it's hard to get a picture of what's on THE OTHER SIDE. In the case of the verse above, Jesus and His disciples were crossing a lake at night when a violent storm erupted in THE MIDDLE of their journey. The storm was so bad that the disciples feared for their lives. The disciples awakened Jesus from His sleep, He arose and rebuked the storm with the words "Peace, be still" and then rebuked His disciples for their lack of faith. They made it to THE OTHER SIDE but what happened in THE MIDDLE of their journey helped them discover some important things about themselves and about their Master.

Friends, we are on a journey in life. The goal is to get to THE OTHER SIDE. THE OTHER SIDE is awesome and glorious, but right smack dab in THE MIDDLE of our journey we run into things that try to steal our peace and joy. There are storms and battles. I bet if we could interview the disciples on THE OTHER SIDE of the lake they would have admitted it was silly for them to get so disturbed about the storm they went through after seeing what Jesus was able to do using a simple rebuke from His lips. I have a feeling that when we get to the THE OTHER SIDE of where we're going we will also be a little embarrassed about how worried and fretful we were while in THE MIDDLE of our journey here on Earth.

So, here's your encouragement for today. You're going to make it to THE OTHER SIDE! Don't freak out about what's happening in THE MIDDLE of the journey. When you get to THE OTHER SIDE everything that happened in THE MIDDLE will just be a fleeting memory.

MY CONFESSION FOR TODAY:
No matter what happens to me in THE MIDDLE of my journey I won't take my eyes off of Jesus…I won't worry, fret, fear or "throw in the towel" because I know what awaits me on THE OTHER SIDE.

Revelation 21:4
He will wipe away every tear from their eyes, and death will be no more nor mourning nor crying nor pain; they will be no more, because the former things [the things that happened in THE MIDDLE] *have passed away."*

WHATCHA CATCHIN'?
May 5 | November 2

While strolling along the banks of Smith Lake one foggy Saturday morning I saw an older gentleman fishing from his boat, close to shore. He was engaged in a fight, trying to reel in a fairly good-sized fish. I watched with interest to see what kind of fish he was struggling with. As the fish got closer to the boat the man's reel bent to the point that it seemed it would snap in two from the weight and pull of the monster he had on the line. Finally he got it reeled in. It was a beautiful large-mouth bass. I'm guessing it must have weighed three or four pounds. I called out "That's a nice-looking fish!" He replied, "Yeah, but it's not what I'm fishing for... I'm fishing for crappie," and he unhooked the lunker and threw him back in the lake.

Now I'll be honest. If I were to catch a bass that size I probably would have had it stuffed and mounted, and people would have had to suffer through hearing me brag about the catch for months to come. But here's a guy who wasn't interested in the size and weight of the fish, because it wasn't the kind of fish he was looking for. Crappie aren't nearly as impressive in size or weight... but if that's what you want out of your fishing experience, nothing else can take its place.

In life, people have different things that they are looking for. Some are looking to achieve "big" things that are impressive and that catch people's attention. Others may stumble upon "big" things in their life but that's not their motivation for living... they're looking for something that goes beyond "size and weight." They're looking for something specific that adds meaning to their life. It doesn't have to be big, shiny and impressive... it just has to bring peace, contentment and fulfillment.

The longer I live the more I've come to realize "All that glitters is not gold." You can have the glitz and glamour of Hollywood... you can have the athletic fame of the NFL or NBA... you can have the financial gain of Wall Street, and still not be satisfied with what you've found. True contentment can't be found in what this world offers. When you catch it, throw it back... don't have it stuffed and mounted... don't boast and brag of your exploits. It only brings temporary happiness. True contentment can only be found when a person looks in the direction of Heaven, to the One Who had a specific purpose in mind when He created us to fellowship with Him and to please Him. Yes, that's when a person finds what they're looking for in this life... a meaningful relationship with their Maker.

DEALING WITH CONFUSION
May 6 | November 3

For God is not the author of confusion, but of peace, as in all churches of the saints. - 1 Corinthians 14:33 (KJV)

This verse has helped me many times throughout my life. Whenever I see confusion break out concerning simple, foundational truths that I find in God's Word I know one thing for certain… God did not AUTHOR it. The verse above tells us that He is the Author of Peace. That only leaves one of two authors who create confusion… man or Satan. Can I tell you today that if you're confused about truths that are firmly established in God's Word, that confusion is not from God… guaranteed. He wouldn't have included the scripture verse above in His Word if He wanted to bring clarity to us through confusion.

Don't make decisions about what you believe when you are confused. If you are confused, confess it to God and ask Him to shed light on the darkness that is shrouding you and keeping you from seeing the truth. Decisions about what you believe should only be made when you've thoroughly considered TRUTH… not feelings, or emotions, or experiences.

Confusion is just like an illness. It can only be cured by applying TRUTH. Those who refuse to listen to truth remain in their illness. The illness is contagious. One confused person who speaks passionately and authoritatively from their position of confusion can be quite persuasive… especially if those who are listening are not firmly grounded in TRUTH themselves.

Confusion exists where TRUTH is ignored, or not known. If you're feeling confused I strongly suggest that you take large portions of time to read the New Testament, where the basis for TRUTH is found in Jesus Christ. He wants to heal confusion. He reminds us "The TRUTH will set you free." In the garden of Gethsemane he prayed for his future disciples by saying "Sanctify them by the TRUTH; YOUR WORD IS TRUTH." Jesus told us the source of TRUTH when He was praying to His Father…. GOD'S WORD IS TRUTH. When we accept and follow the TRUTH found in God's Word, confusion will have to cease as it gives way to the Author of Peace.

Romans 3:4 (KJV)
Let God be true, but every man a liar.

THIS LITTLE LIGHT OF MINE
May 7 | November 4

I woke up one morning at 5:30am and walked to my desk in the dark. I noticed a beam of blue light coming from my desk that I've never noticed before. The cabinet door to my modem was slightly ajar and the blue lights that flicker on it let off enough light to illuminate a beautiful little blue shaft of light in the dark room. It's unfortunate that it stays closed inside a cabinet all day long... its light is rarely seen. I thought about that saying of Jesus, "Neither do men light a candle and put it under a bushel" (Matthew 5:15). Light was created to be seen. It was the very first thing that God created when He made the Earth. I almost felt sorry for the little blue light on my modem so I opened the cabinet door, letting it illuminate more than just the little cramped space inside the cabinet. I gave it a chance to do the thing it was created to do... I gave it a chance to shine!

Let me tell you about another little light I feel sorry for... the refrigerator light. Talk about hiding your light! Poor little thing is constantly hidden. No one ever gives it any thought at all... until they want a glass of milk, or slice of cheese. Just think about that little light for a minute. It's whole purpose in this life is to shine only for a moment... when you open the refrigerator door. The rest of its life it hides in obscurity behind the closed doors of the refrigerator. No, it doesn't stay "on" all the time. If it did, perhaps it would feel a little more successful in its life. The only time it gets a chance to shine is when you are hungry. But aren't you glad it's there! My refrigerator light went out last year and it took me a couple of days to get a new bulb, so for days we had no light in our refrigerator. I'd open the door and couldn't see what I was wanting to eat... is that a jar of jelly? Nope, it's a jar of dill pickles! I didn't realize how much I loved that little light until it was no longer shining.

So, today, I salute all those little lights in our lives. The unsung heroes in our dark world. Yes, it truly is a dark world out there, brothers and sisters. But you were created for such a time as this. Maybe you think your "little" light won't have much impact, but the darker the darkness is, the brighter your light shines. The world is not only dark, it's also hungry. Let your light shine on Jesus so a hungry world can see the One they are truly hungry for.

THE LORD IS YOUR KEEPER
May 8 | November 5

Psalm 121:5 (English Standard Version)
The LORD is your KEEPER; The LORD is your shade on your right hand.

We believe in God's "Saving Power" to save us from our sins and secure a place in Heaven for us. We believe in God's "Delivering Power" to deliver us from the troubles and problems of life. But, do we believe in God's "Keeping Power"? Do we believe that He is constantly keeping us away from trouble, protecting us, guarding us, keeping evil at bay?

Is "keeping" important to God? I'll answer that question with another question. What was the first job that God gave Adam in the garden? Was it not to "tend and KEEP" the garden of Eden? To protect it, guard it, and keep trouble out of it? Didn't all of our trouble begin when Adam failed to KEEP the garden of Eden protected from a deceptive serpent? And, after man fell, still having a command from God to be a "keeper," the sinful Cain replied to God's question of the whereabouts of his brother Abel with the snide remark "Am I my brother's KEEPER?"

Yes, KEEPING is important to God (even if it isn't to man). So, be mindful today that God is KEEPING you. He doesn't just want to SAVE you and DELIVER you from trouble… He wants to KEEP you away from trouble and evil. It's a job that He takes very seriously. Trust God's KEEPING power over your life, today.

Psalm 140:4 (NIV)
KEEP me safe, LORD, from the hands of the wicked; protect me from the violent, who devise ways to trip my feet.

Numbers 6:24 (KJV)
The LORD bless thee, and KEEP thee.

Isaiah 42:6 (KJV)
I the LORD have called thee in righteousness, and will hold thine hand, and will KEEP thee.

Isaiah 26:3 (KJV)
Thou wilt KEEP him in perfect peace, whose mind is stayed on thee.

GOODNESS AND MERCY

May 9 | November 6

"The Lord is GOOD and His MERCY endureth forever." I know that I've said that phrase at least a couple hundred times in the last few years. The phrase is repeated throughout the Bible dozens of times. Funny thing... even though I've said it and read it over and over again, I discovered new level of meaning to it just recently. It hit me that GOODNESS is manifested by MERCY. In other words, one of the reasons why God is so GOOD is because He is MERCIFUL. If it still hasn't registered with you what I'm saying, I'll say it this way: If you claim to be a GOOD person but you don't show MERCY to others, you are lying. You can't be GOOD without being MERCIFUL... the two are eternally connected.

Psalm 23, the most-loved chapter of the Bible, ends with the phrase "Surely GOODNESS and MERCY shall follow me all the days of my life... Micah 6:8 tells us, "He has shown thee, O man, what is GOOD, and what does the Lord require of thee but to do justly and to love MERCY...." Did you catch that? God wants us to LOVE MERCY! Why did Jesus give the Pharisees such a hard time during His earthly ministry? Because they claimed to be GOOD but they showed no MERCY. There is no GOODNESS where there is no MERCY. He rebuked them with these words, "Woe to you, scribes and Pharisees, hypocrites! For you tithe mint and dill and cummin, and have neglected the weightier provisions of the law, justice and MERCY and faithfulness" (Matthew 23:23).

Friends, I don't know if you consider yourself to be a GOOD person or not. If you do, take a look at the amount of MERCY you have toward others. If it is rarely (or never) shown it may be time to re-evaluate the meaning of the word GOODNESS.

Psalm 100:5 (KJV)
For the Lord is GOOD; His MERCY is everlasting.

1 Chronicles 16:34 (KJV)
O give thanks to the LORD, for He is good; For His lovingkindness is everlasting.

Ezra 3:11 (KJV)
And they sang together by course in praising and giving thanks unto the LORD; because he is good, for his mercy endureth for ever.

DEFEAT YOUR KIDNEY STONES!
May 10 | November 7

In October of 2017 I suffered through the worst pain I've experienced in my lifetime… a kidney stone. When I finally passed that kidney stone I was amazed by how something so very small could create such gigantic pain. You might think this is strange, but I actually kept the kidney stone as a weird kind of "keepsake" to remember my ordeal. I taped the little stone (it's only slightly bigger than a granule of salt) to a white piece of paper, and I keep it on a shelf near my desk. I look at it from time to time and marvel at the fact that little thing brought me to my knees in pain.

In Christian circles, we talk about "facing and defeating our giants." Everybody loves that kind of motivating teaching. We envision ourselves as "David" and that big giant is out there breathing out threats against us, but we run courageously into battle to defeat him! That kind of talk really does "pump us up." And, if we by chance lose our battle against a giant, everyone understands… after all, it was a giant, and I'm just "little ol' me."

But, to be honest, we don't face giants everyday. Dealing with giants is kind of a rare life event for most of us. The thing we face most often in our life is a whole lot of "kidney stones" … tiny, little things that try to steal our faith and joy… tiny, little things that cause us pain, discomfort and inconvenience… tiny, little things that build upon one another, day after day until they feel more like boulders than tiny little grains of sand. I'm not embarrassed to tell you I've been defeated by a few giants in my lifetime, but I'm ashamed to admit that I've been defeated by a kidney stone on more than one occasion… and I'm not talking about the one I passed back in 2017, either.

Song of Solomon 2:15 reminds us that it's the "little foxes that spoil the vine." Terry Talbot wrote a song in the 70s that included this thought, "It's not the mountain ahead that wears you down with dread… it's the grain of sand still in your shoe." So, I'll leave you with this encouragement today: Don't concern yourself with giants today… just make sure you defeat your kidney stones!

Luke 16:10 (NAS)
He who is faithful in a very little thing is faithful also in much

THE ROOT, THE SHOOT & THE FRUIT
May 11 | November 8

I was teaching a Bible Study on Anger for a group of men. We read from Genesis 4 about the very first murder in history: Cain murdering his brother, Abel. I made mention that the initial cause of Cain's anger was jealousy. So the process that took place went like this: Cain was jealous of his brother, the jealousy grew into anger, and the anger grew into murder.

Listen, a person doesn't turn into a murderer overnight, just like a seed doesn't grow into a plant overnight. There's a process that takes place. First there's a ROOT, then there's a SHOOT, and then there's the FRUIT. That's the way all things in our lives are produced… both good and bad. If you won't uproot jealousy in your life it will eventually push its way through to the surface of your life as anger. If you won't weed out the anger in your life you're just a step away from doing something unthinkable, like murder.

You think your jealousy and anger are harmlessly contained within you… that's not true. Roots produce shoots, and shoots produce fruits… it's a fact of Nature. Uproot the jealousy in your life!

Hebrews 12:15 (KJV)
"...lest any root of bitterness (ROOT) springing up trouble you (SHOOT), and thereby many be defiled (FRUIT)"

IN A GARDEN

In a garden the problem began.
Eden the place and Adam the man.
God put him there, gave a single command,
But man disobeyed, from the garden was banned.

In a garden the solution came.
Gethsemane the place, Jesus the name.
Could have disobeyed, but He overcame,
"Not my will but Yours" was his refrain.

Because He obeyed we've received pardon.
Hearts can be soft which once were hardened.
To the one who believes, Eden's restarting,
Thanks to the One who prayed in the garden.

PRAYER SEEDS
May 12 | November 9

Praying is like planting seeds. When you pray you're planting a seed for the future. Seeds don't grow into plants overnight. The seed germinates under the soil and the process is UNSEEN for days, weeks, and sometimes even months before anything appears above ground. People who believe in prayer understand that things are happening in an unseen realm because they planted a seed of prayer. Eventually the seed will produce something in the SEEN realm but you've got to trust that something's happening in the UNSEEN realm first.

You and I are reaping today what we sowed weeks, months and years ago in prayer. That's one of the reasons why Paul told us to "Pray without ceasing" because by doing so we're constantly planting seeds for our future.

Don't be discouraged if you're not seeing immediate results from the prayers that you are presently praying… by faith and patience you will SEE the results when the seed has grown!

Hebrews 6:12 (NIV)
We do not want you to become lazy, but to imitate those who through faith and patience inherit what has been promised.

Mark 4:26-27 (NAS)
The kingdom of God is like a man who casts seed upon the soil; and he goes to bed at night and gets up by day, and the seed sprouts and grows— how, he himself does not know.

TURN WORRY TO PRAYER

Most people think that the amount of time spent worrying about another person (concerned about their physical or spiritual condition) is equal to the amount of love you have for them. But really, it is equal to the amount of time you haven't spent praying for them.

Philippians 4:6 (NLT)
Don't worry about anything; instead, pray about everything. Tell God what you need, and thank him for all he has done.

IT'S "STUCK" IN MY HEAD!
May 13 | November 10

My son and I were sitting at our computers working in my office, and I started singing the Chipmunk's song "Christmas Don't Be Late." About ten or fifteen minutes later my son spoke up, "Thanks a lot Dad! Now I've got that song stuck in my head!" Evidently, he'd been singing that song inside his head for several minutes. HaHa! Well, I didn't necessarily plan on making that happen, but isn't it interesting how a simple tune like that can get stuck in your head and replay itself over and over again? Now, I can think of a lot worse things that could have gotten "stuck" in my son's head, so if I'm going to be the perpetuator of "subliminal mind control" I'm glad it was an innocent, silly song like that one.

Do you realize the power you have to influence other people's thoughts with your words? Some people are very aware of it, and use it to their own advantage. They use words to manipulate people, to get them to do what they want them to do. But, just as much as this power can be used in a negative way, it can also be used in a good way. When we speak words of encouragement, hope, and peace they can get "stuck" in people's minds. People can replay those words of encouragement over and over again in their minds, and it lifts them up, even after we've left the room. Now, let me make this clear… I don't want to manipulate anyone's thinking. But, knowing that this does happen, whether we realize it or not, I'm determined that I will be one who will use this power for good in my life and the lives of those around me. How about you?

The rest of the story? I was driving home from Decatur later that same week (during the Christmas season) and the Chipmunk's song came on the radio. What did I do? I called my son on his cell phone and played the song on the radio for him… I guess sometimes I can be a little bit devious after all!

Proverbs 18:21 (NAS)
Death and life are in the power of the tongue, And those who love it will eat its fruit.

Ephesians 4:29 (KJV)
Let no corrupt communication proceed out of your mouth, but that which is good to the use of edifying, that it may minister grace unto the hearers.

THE NEW GUY
May 14 | November 11

he Bible Study at the Men's Home was over. I was gathering my things to
ead out the door when one of the guys handed me a note. The note said,
"Please pray for the new guy." I looked at the guy that handed me the note
nd asked "Right now? Or just pray for him when I think about him?" He
aid "Right now." So, I waited as he went to get the "new guy."

his "new guy" had just come to New Life Men's Home that day. I knew
e was there because of an addiction but I had no idea what his story
might be. All of the men at the home have struggled with addictions and
he resulting failures and defeats from not being able to overcome them.
As the "new guy" came back to the room I asked him if we could pray for
im. He nodded in humble agreement.

o, how do you pray for someone that you've never met before, that you
lon't know anything about? You trust God to give you the right words. As
 began to pray for this broken man, God gave me the exact words that
eeded to be said to bring him encouragement. It went something like this:

"Today, you are walking through a doorway... the old door is closing
behind you. All of the things that you've done up to this point in time
are behind you. Your failures and defeats. The darkness, the pain and
the hurt. The hurt that you've felt and the hurt that you've caused
others. You can't go back through that doorway. You know what's
there and there's nothing for you but pain there. But a NEW door
is opening in front of you. This doorway leads to light, meaning,
purpose, fellowship, new friendships, prosperity, success and God's
plan for your life. There's no mistake that you are here at NEW LIFE
Men's Home... because you are starting a NEW LIFE from here...
old things have passed away... all things have become NEW for you."

looked up at the "new guy" and tears were streaming down his face.
God's Holy Spirit had touched his heart. I hugged him and his tears were
bsorbed into my jacket... tears of repentance... tears of joy for a fresh
tart and a NEW chance at life.

The next morning, I thought again about the note that was handed to me.
"Please pray for the new guy." How prophetic that note was. For, truly...
e became a NEW GUY as we prayed for him that night!

DID GOD REALLY SAY...?
May 15 | November 12

In Genesis 2 God's words to Adam were, "You are free to eat from any tree in the garden; but you must not eat from the tree of the knowledge of good and evil." Now, the very first recorded words of Satan in the Bible are "DID GOD REALLY SAY you shall not eat from any tree in the garden?" He caused Adam and Eve to doubt the word of God... the clear instructions that God had given them just days earlier.

Now, let's move ahead to the New Testament, to the day that Jesus was baptized. The Bible says that the Holy Spirit came on Jesus in the bodily form of a dove and God's voice spoke with these words, "YOU ARE MY BELOVED SON, in you I am well-pleased." Just a few days after this glorious moment Jesus was being tempted in the wilderness by Satan. What were Satan's words to Jesus? "IF YOU ARE THE SON OF GOD command that these stones be made bread." I've capitalized the first part of His words to highlight something important here. You see, Satan was trying to get Jesus to doubt the "word of God" that He had heard at His baptism just days earlier. (Just like he tried to get Adam and Eve to doubt the word of God that they had heard.) It was as if he was saying "DID GOD REALLY SAY You are His son? If so, prove it!"

So you can see that Satan's number one tactic in tempting us is to get us to doubt the word of God, the clear instruction and direction that God has given us. He attacks our current society with these words every day. Just fill in the blank... "Did God really say that _____ is a sin?"

Not only does Satan want us to doubt the commands of God, he also wants us to doubt the promises of God. "Did God really say 'You can do all things through Christ who gives you strength?'" "Did God really say 'By Jesus' stripes you are healed?'" "Did God really say 'You are the righteousness of God?'" etc. etc. When you hear a voice inside yourself that causes you to doubt the words God has spoken, know for certain that you're hearing the same voice Adam heard in the Garden of Eden... "Did God really say...."

2 Corinthians 2:11 (NAS)
That no advantage would be taken of us by Satan, for we are not ignorant of his schemes.

DEATH BY CONSTRICTION
May 16 | November 13

Satan came to Adam and Eve in the form of a serpent in the Garden of Eden. If you know much about serpents you know that most species kill their prey by constriction… wrapping their coils around the victims and squeezing their life's breath out of them. How fitting that Satan is symbolized by a serpent.

Satan saw the lump of clay that God fashioned into the first man, Adam. That lump of clay was limp and lifeless until the moment God breathed LIFE into his nostrils. Satan saw that the life of the man was in the breath that the Almighty imparted to him. So, what does he do? He tries to SQUEEZE us, to squeeze the LIFE out of us. What is STRESS, PRESSURE and ANXIETY? It is the coils of our adversary wrapping around us attempting to squeeze the breath of God out of us.

I found the following information on the internet at *https://www.cardiosmart.org*:

> Stress can cause shortness of breath or make it worse. Once you start feeling short of breath, it is common to get nervous or anxious. This can make your shortness of breath even worse.
>
> Being anxious tightens the muscles that help you breathe, and this makes you start to breathe faster. As you get more anxious, your breathing muscles get tired. This causes even more shortness of breath and more anxiety. At this point, you may panic.

Yes, even science and the medical community agree on this. Stress creates shortness of breath. Many have had full-fledged panic attacks caused directly from this shortness of breath. Remember, this is nothing more than the serpent's coils constricting your breathing… trying to steal the breath of God that gives you life. Rebuke and resist stress and anxiety from your life every time you feel the weight of it… it is a tactic of your enemy to squeeze the life out of you.

Job 33:4 (NIV)
The Spirit of God has made me; the breath of the Almighty gives me life.

JUPITER
May 17 | November 14

Jupiter. It's the largest planet in our solar system. Thirteen hundred Earths could fit inside it. It's enormous! But oddly enough, I never think about it. It never comes into my thoughts. I don't think about it on a daily basis. I don't think about it once a week, or even once a month. It's not in any of my thoughts (except for today in this devotional thought). Yet the fact that I don't think about it doesn't take away from its existence or its enormity. It doesn't reduce in size because of my failure to consider it in my thoughts. I don't take anything away from it by ignoring the fact of its existence. It remains and endures regardless of the attention and focus that I give it. It doesn't need to prove its existence to me. It doesn't need to prove its enormous size to me. If I choose to ignore it my whole life, still it would remain in orbit around the sun. Still it would hold the honor of being our solar system's largest planet.

God. He created Jupiter, and our solar system, and the universe. He is enormous in scale. He would have to be in order to create the great expanse of the universe. He exists and endures throughout generations. My consideration and contemplation of Him (or lack thereof) doesn't add to Him or take away from Him. He doesn't grow when I think about Him or reduce in size if I don't. If I ignore Him He continues to exist. If I deny His existence it doesn't make Him less real. If I never think about Him, if the thought of Him never crosses my mind, it doesn't detract from Him in any way. He doesn't need to prove Himself or explain Himself any more than He already has. On the contrary, we are the ones who should prove ourselves to Him!

Man is kind of funny. He comes up with sayings like, "If a tree falls in the forest and no one is around to hear it, does it make a sound?" We think our awareness of something is what makes the thing or person real. But you know what? It doesn't matter one little bit if we choose to believe in God or deny Him. Our belief or lack thereof doesn't change Him in any way. He is God... and always will be.

Isaiah 43:13 (NLT)
From eternity to eternity I am God. No one can snatch anyone out of my hand. No one can undo what I have done.

JUDGE NOT
May 18 | November 15

Judge not, and you will not be judged. Condemn not, and you will not be condemned. Forgive, and you will be forgiven." - (Luke 6:37)

There are three kinds of "wrong" that a person can commit.
1. Wrong against God
2. Wrong against others
3. Wrong against us personally

When a person commits a wrong against God, we are tempted to commit a wrong against them… it's called judgement.

When a person commits a wrong against another person, we are tempted to commit a wrong against them… it's called condemnation.

When a person commits a wrong against us personally, we will be tempted to commit a wrong against them… it's called unforgiveness.

You've heard the saying before, "Two wrongs don't make a right" haven't you? We will never turn a wrong around by committing a wrong ourselves. The way we respond to wrongs committed against God, against others and against ourselves will be the way others (and God) will respond to us when we commit wrongs. It's a "cause and effect" relationship that God set in motion when He created the world. It is the same "cause and effect" relationship that exists when we plant a seed in the ground and get a plant out of it. It's called "reaping what you sow."

MY PRAYER FOR TODAY:
"Father, help me to obey the words of Jesus found in Luke 6:37. When people do You wrong, help me to not get offended on Your behalf. When I get offended on Your behalf it always turns into judgement. I know that You are forgiving and merciful to those who do YOU wrong. Help me to be forgiving and merciful to those who do ME wrong. If others choose to do wrong that is their decision... I choose not to perpetuate the wrong with my own wrong response. Help me Lord! In Jesus' name I pray."

Matthew 6:15 (NIV)
But if you do not forgive others their sins, your Father will not forgive your sins.

A TWO-WAY RELATIONSHIP
May 19 | November 16

When I was a kid I was painfully shy. I remember in Junior High School there was this girl I liked from afar, but I was so shy I never spoke to her. I never actually came within three feet of her. Yet, I called her my girlfriend. I even told a few friends that she was my girlfriend. We never held hands, much less kissed. I made one gesture that solidified the relationship in my mind… I bought her a bracelet for Christmas. But, did I give the gift to her myself? No. I had a friend do it for me.

So there I was thinking I was "in a relationship" with this girl that I never spoke to, never came close to, never held hands with, and never kissed. I thought we had something special! But, if you had asked her, "Are you Greg's girlfriend" she most likely would have replied, "Greg who?"

In order to have a "relationship" it's necessary to have some form of contact or communication. If you don't understand this you can fool yourself into thinking you've got something that you really don't have… just like my "relationship" with that girl.

There are a lot of people these days who say they're in a relationship with Jesus Christ. They might mention His name in conversation, they may even go to church regularly. But a true relationship is not established by saying a person's name or even by being in the same room with that person. A true relationship is found in personal one-on-one contact.

It's embarrassing to be in a one-way relationship when you're thinking it's actually two-way. In the case of a relationship with the Lord, it can not only be embarrassing, it can actually be eternally detrimental, as can be seen in the following verse of scripture: "Not everyone who says to Me, 'Lord, Lord,' will enter the kingdom of heaven, but only he who does the will of My Father in heaven. Many will say to Me on that day, 'Lord, Lord, did we not prophesy in Your name, and in Your name drive out demons and perform many miracles?' Then I will tell them plainly, 'I never knew you; depart from Me, you workers of lawlessness.'" - Matthew 7:21-23

Jesus said, "I never KNEW you." In other words, "We weren't in a relationship." Listen, you might participate in church activities and give your time and money to the Lord. You might even perform miracles. But nothing can replace the most important part of the Christian experience... a personal, two-way relationship with the Lord Jesus Christ.

IT TAKES A THIEF
May 20 | November 17

Here's a thought you should consider,
Though it may sound rather odd,
"It takes a thief to show us all
How much we're loved by God."
For on the cross, at Calvary's Hill
The place where Jesus died,
A vile thief, paid for his crimes
He was hung by Jesus' side.
We know nothing of this man
Except he was a thief.
He robbed, he stole from others,
He caused such pain and grief.
On the cross, it seemed to all,
"He gets what he deserved!
He's finally paying for his crimes,
Now, justice has been served!"
But in his final moments
As he hung upon that tree,
He turned to Jesus by his side
And said "Lord, Remember me!"
Without pause, or hesitation
And, without thinking twice,
Jesus told the thief, "Today,
You'll be with me in Paradise."
If you think that you're unworthy
Of all God's love and favor,
The truth is you are right, my friend,
That's why you need a Savior!"
You're unworthy on your own
But if "in Christ" your life is hid
You won't get what **YOU** deserve
Because that's what Jesus did.
He loves you, makes you worthy
And though it sounds beyond belief,
If you should ever doubt it,
Think about that dying thief.

TWO WAYS OF SEEING THINGS
May 21 | November 18

Take a close look at the word DIVISION. The first part of the word is DI which means TWO, TWICE or DOUBLE in the Greek language. The second part of the word is VISION which we all know means "the ability to see." So, why is there so much DIVISION all around us? Simple... because there are TWO WAYS OF SEEING THINGS.

One person sees a child within the womb of its mother as a human being that has rights, and should be protected... another person sees it as part of the woman's body, and that the woman has rights that should be protected. Thus DIVISION exists (TWO WAYS OF SEEING THINGS).

So, the question must be asked "Who is seeing things the RIGHT WAY?" All of us have the ability to SEE things in the RIGHT WAY on occasion but we also have the ability to SEE things in the WRONG WAY, too. Since none of us are perfect we can't rely on any other human being's ability to see things in the RIGHT WAY on every single subject. So what can we do? We've got to trust someone other than another human... Someone who sees things in the RIGHT WAY on every subject that exists... Someone who has never erred in any of their judgements or decisions... Someone who sees things from the right perspective. We all know that there is only One who fits that description, and that is God Himself.

It's kind of a bummer to have to admit this, but DIVISION will always exist as long as there are TWO WAYS OF SEEING THINGS. No one is going to change the way they SEE things just because the government tells them to, or just because the church tells them to. But, here's a novel idea... What if God tells us to change the WAY we SEE things? Would you and I change for Him? If everyone could see things from God's perspective, DIVISION would end... for, then everyone would be able to see things **THE RIGHT WAY.**

(P.S. Reading the Bible is a very good way to discover the WAY that God SEES things.)

Proverbs 14:12 (NAS)
There is a way which seems right to a man, But its end is the way of death.

FORGIVE US OUR DEBTS
May 22 | November 19

Several years ago there was a man who owed me a few hundred dollars for some work I did for him, and he never paid me. Months went by and the guy seemed to be avoiding me. The matter was further complicated by the fact that this man was a Christian brother. Now, usually I can be pretty forgiving, but the debt that was owed to me began to weigh on me, probably because I was a young father and we were "pinching pennies" at the time while spending all of our money on diapers and formula. I confided in two of my closest friends about my dilemma and, to be honest, I spoke badly of the Christian man that owed me the money. In other words I used my friends' ears as garbage cans to "trash" the man.

Several months went by and I eventually forgot about the debt altogether. But, one night this man came up to me, handed me the money he owed me, and asked me to forgive him as he stood there weeping. Wow. It was such a humbling moment for him to approach me the way he did. I could tell his desire for forgiveness was genuine. All of a sudden I was convicted in my heart for the ill will that I had toward him. I gave him a hug and told him that I forgave him… then I started weeping. (When forgiveness is real it's usually more than "just words.") I told him that I didn't want the money, but he refused to take it back.

When we parted, I looked down at the money in my hand… the money that had made me angry… the money that had made me unforgiving… the money that had caused me to slander my Christian brother. God spoke to my heart, and I knew what I had to do.

I immediately called my two friends to meet with them. I asked them to forgive me for dishonoring and disrespecting the man who owed me the money, as I slandered his name in front of them on a couple of occasions. I then took the money that had been given to me just a few minutes earlier and split it between the two of them… that's what I felt like God had told me to do as recompense for my behavior. I guess you could call it a sacrifice, but the money was no good to me. I better understood the meaning of the Lord's prayer when Jesus said "forgive us our DEBTS as we forgive our DEBTORS."

Forgiveness says "YOU DON'T OWE ME ANYTHING."

HAPPINESS
May 23 | November 20

I took my dog, Archie, for a walk right before sunset. I let him off his leash so he could run free in a large, fenced-in area. You should have seen him! He ran like he was at the Kentucky Derby. By the way he was accelerating I thought he was running after a bird, squirrel or rabbit at first, but then he looped back towards me at full-speed, turned a flip, and began rolling around in the grass. He was just having fun! I couldn't help but laugh out loud and smile. That simple little moment of seeing him enjoy himself made me happy.

After that moment passed, I wondered about this emotion we call "happiness." Scientists tell us that the physiological reason we experience the feeling of happiness is due to a release of hormones, called endorphins, in our brains. Scientists are so smart! They've systematically relegated all of our emotions, feelings, and dreams to chemical and neurological functions within our bodies. You're not actually "happy"… you're just experiencing a chemical reaction within your brain. Scientifically speaking, they are correct, but there are things that happen in our soul and spirit that can't always be scientifically explained.

I think about the happiness I felt on the inside as I watched my dog enjoying himself. Was it just an endorphin rush that I was experiencing? Or, could it be that there is a Creator who Himself is a happy, joy-filled Being, who put within me the ability to experience His happiness even in the smallest of things? 1 Timothy 6:17 says that God richly provides us with all things to enjoy. Joy is an emotion and sensation that has been passed down to us by our Maker. It is one of the benefits of being connected to His kingdom, to be able to find a rich enjoyment in life that doesn't have to be scrutinized or questioned by scientific reasoning. And, just as much as I myself experienced pure happiness by seeing my dog having fun, I can't help but believe that God Himself is blessed and made happy when He sees His children enjoying the life that they've been given.

God has blessed us with a little foretaste of Heaven each time we experience joy and happiness here on Earth. "Thank you God for this wonderful appetizer called JOY!"

1 Timothy 6:17 (NLT)
Their trust should be in God, who richly gives us all we need for our enjoyment.

TWO REBUKES
May 24 | November 21

Jesus was asleep in the stern of the boat as the disciples fought to keep that boat afloat during a terrible storm at sea (Matthew 8). They woke Jesus up with the words, "Save us Lord! We are perishing?" Jesus wiped the sleep from His eyes and rebuked the disciples for their lack of faith with the words, "Why are you afraid, you men of little faith?" Then He also rose and rebuked the winds and the waves. In an instant, the storm was calmed. The disciples were amazed by the authority their Master possesssed.

When you look closely at that scripture passage in Matthew 8, you discover that Jesus had two words of rebuke on that day. The first one was directed towards people who were stirred up by fear. The second one was directed towards a storm that was stirred up by wind.

A storm is a "stirring"… an agitation of the elements. Wind stirs up clouds, which bump into one another sparking lightning and thunder. Fear is also a "stirring"… an agitation of our thoughts. Our thoughts stir up worry, doubt, and lots of negative energy.

Fear is a hindrance to our faith. So, before you rebuke the storms in your life, rebuke the fear.

LOVE... AND TRUTH

How important is love? 1 John 4:8 says that "God is love." So, love is so important that God is known by the name LOVE. Now, here's another question…How important is truth? In John 14:6 Jesus called Himself "The way, the TRUTH and the life." The TRUTH is so important that Jesus is called "The TRUTH." So, God is LOVE... Jesus is TRUTH.

Yes, there's no denying the importance of LOVE. But, TRUTH is equally important. If it wasn't, Jesus wouldn't have called Himself by that name. So, I will continue to show people LOVE, but I will also continue to tell people TRUTH. I will not surrender TRUTH for the sake of LOVE… just like I wouldn't give up Jesus so I could keep God… that's an impossibility.

John 8:32
And ye shall know the truth, and the truth shall make you free.

PUSH THROUGH
May 25 | November 22

It had been a rough and stressful day leading up to the time when I was to leave for the Monday Night Bible Study at the Men's Home. I had almost considered calling them to say I wasn't coming, but I knew I needed to push through my own small problems if I was going to help these men with their much larger problems. (Many of these men were struggling with alcohol and drug addictions and trying to stay out of prison.)

When I got to the Home, there was a heated argument going on in another room. The argument was preventing our Bible Study from beginning. The argument began to die down just a little, and one of the guys said to me "Greg, maybe you should just come back tomorrow." So there I was, with a decision to make. The stress of the day almost kept me from coming, and now this heated argument was preventing me from conducting the Bible Study. Then, from deep inside me, a boldness came over me. I began to pray out loud over the volatile situation that was taking place, remembering the words of Jesus as He spoke to the storm at sea… "Peace, Be Still!" Within a minute the argument ceased, the Bible Study started, and I shared a word about RESTORATION.

I shared with those men that Jesus didn't just die so they could go to Heaven one day… He died to RESTORE them back to His original plan for them. He wanted to give them back all that they had lost through their ignorance, sin and rebellion. He wanted to give back to them all that the devil stole from them as they went down the wrong pathway.

When the Bible Study was over one of the guys came up to me privately and said, "Greg, pray for me…I'm a fallen minister…I lost my church because of alcoholism. I lost the respect of the people that I ministered to. I don't know if I can be restored or not." Then it hit me… this man was the reason for the message God gave me about restoration. He was the reason I had to push through my stressful day to come to the Men's Home. He was the reason I had to push through the awkwardness of that heated argument. Had I not pushed through, he wouldn't have heard about God's willingness to RESTORE him. I prayed with the man and told him that God could still use him in His service.

Friend, there are people out there who need to hear from God, and you might be the very person that has God's Word for them. PUSH THROUGH your struggles so you can help other people PUSH THROUGH theirs.

NEVER STOP PRAYING!
May 26 | November 23

A few years ago, a friend of mine asked me to pray for his business. He asked me to specifically pray for his equipment. I did as he requested and prayed diligently for a couple of days. A few days later, he called me and asked, "Have you been praying for my business and my equipment?" I replied with a wholehearted, "Yes!" To which he replied, "Well stop it! Two of my main pieces of equipment broke down this week." He said it kind of jokingly, but to be honest, it felt like a "prayer failure."

What do you do when you've prayed and it doesn't seem to be working? An even better question would be: "What do you do when you've prayed and the situation actually gets worse?" Should you stop praying? Could prayer actually make matters worse? Does the Bible tell us what to do when our prayers don't appear to be working?

I was thinking along these lines on my morning walk one day. You see, I had been praying for someone who was in the hospital. I was praying for healing, comfort and peace to be with them. A few minutes after praying for the person I got a text message that let me know their situation had worsened. Once again, it felt like a "prayer failure." But, then the Lord reminded me of a passage of scripture found in Luke 18. Jesus told a parable about an unjust judge and a widow woman. Luke 18:1 tells us the reason Jesus told the parable: "Then Jesus told his disciples a parable to show them that they should *always pray and not give up.*" Did you catch the significance of the reason Jesus told the parable? He told the parable to remind people to always pray and never give up... NEVER STOP PRAYING.

Just think about that for a minute. There'd be no reason for Jesus to encourage us to "always pray and not give up" if every prayer we prayed was always instantly answered? Listen, lots more people would be praying a lot more often if every single prayer got instant results, wouldn't they? You know it's true! But, Jesus was inferring that there aren't always instant results. And, because of this fact, people might get discouraged when they don't see the results they've prayed for. That was the whole reason for Him telling the parable. I find that very encouraging in the midst of my seeming "prayer failures." No matter the results, I'll never stop praying!

MY SIMPLE PRAYER FOR TODAY:
"Lord, help me to keep on praying, even when it doesn't seem to be working."

YOU DON'T HAVE TO WORK...
BUT YOU'VE GOT TO FIGHT!
May 27 | November 24

In Egypt, the Israelites WORKED and they WORKED HARD... but the never profited from their work because they were slaves... their WORK only benefited their taskmasters. But, when God led them to the Prom ised Land this is what He offered them:

> *"Then it shall come about when the LORD your God brings you into the land which He swore to your fathers, Abraham, Isaac and Jacob, to give you, great and splendid cities which you did not build, and houses full of all good things which you did not fill, and hewn cisterns which you did not dig, vineyards and olive trees which you did not plant, and you eat and are satisfied"*
> *- Deuteronomy 6:10-11 (NAS)*

Yes, God promised to give them things that they did not WORK for. Ther is one detail, though, that you must understand about this proposition Truly, the Israelites did not have to WORK to receive the PROMISE.. but they did have to FIGHT. God told the Israelites that they would hav to fight and conquer the Canaanites in order to receive the benefits of th Promised Land.

Likewise, in the Christian life, we don't have to WORK for our salva tion. We receive God's Promises through the provision of His Grace. But make no mistake, there is a battle that we must FIGHT to apprehend al that God has promised to give us. Grace does not call us to a life of leisur and ease...it gives us strength for the battle.

You don't have to WORK to receive God's Promises...but you do hav to FIGHT!

1 Timothy 6:12 (KJV)
Fight the good fight of faith, lay hold on eternal life, whereunto thou ar also called, and hast professed a good profession before many witnesses.

1 Timothy 1:18 (NIV)
I am giving you this command in keeping with the prophecies once mad about you, so that by recalling them you may fight the battle well.

A BAD CONNECTION
May 28 | November 25

I bought a new High Definition, big screen television for my living room. The picture on the display model at the store looked awesome, but when I got the television set up at my home I was very dissatisfied with the picture quality. At first, I wondered if there might be something wrong with my satellite dish, but everything checked out okay on it. Then I tried tweaking the television settings, but I was still getting a lot of distortion and "noise" in the picture. After going several weeks with inferior picture quality, I was beginning to think the television was defective. I was considering taking it back to the store, but decided to try one last thing. The cable that connected the satellite dish to the television was a cheap, flimsy cable, so I went to the store and bought a new, heavy-duty, high definition coaxial cable to replace it. When I did that the problem was immediately solved. The noise and distortion were gone. The problem wasn't in the television or the satellite dish… it was in the cable that was delivering the signal from the satellite dish to the television.

An important life lesson was learned from this little technical glitch. I discovered that you can have a good transmitter and a good receiver, but if there's a bad connection between the two, the results will be less than ideal. Herein lies a problem that God has had to deal with for centuries with His people. You see, God is perfect, and He speaks to us and tells us His message in hopes that we will share it with a lost and dying world. But, unfortunately, He has to rely on our less-than-perfect ability to communicate and transmit his signal to others. When we communicate His message, many times there is "distortion" and "noise" that is not filtered out due to our less-than-perfect, human nature. Those who hear His message from our lips might begin to wonder about God's character, love, and grace due to the imperfections of those who transmit His message.

God is an awesome God. He is a Transmitter of love, grace and acceptance. Those who speak on His behalf should transmit His message with clarity… without tainted, human interference. But that doesn't always happen. If you have received transmissions of God's message that left you wondering if God is truly good and loving, odds are that you received a faulty transmission through an imperfect signal transmitter (i.e. a Human).

"Lord forgive us when we fail to be good transmitters of Your love, grace and acceptance. In Jesus' Name I pray. Amen."

BLESS THEM... PRAY FOR THEM
May 29 | November 26

Have you ever had the feeling that a certain person didn't like you but you couldn't really figure out why? Such was the case with an acquaintance of mine in recent months. We used to get along just fine, always greeting one another with a handshake or a friendly "hello," but somewhere along the line I must have offended him in some way. I noticed that he became distant and tried his best to avoid me whenever our paths crossed. Although we were never "close" I still didn't like the fact that there was this obvious awkwardness between the two of us. So, what do you do when someone doesn't like you, and you just can't seem to make things right again? That was my question and dilemma.

So, one Monday night I saw this guy again. As he walked through the room I was in, he was heading for the door without speaking to me or acknowledging my presence. I called his name and jokingly said "Do you not like me anymore?" He stopped, looked at me and gave me a couple of excuses for being "distant" toward me... none of which felt like the true reason for his coldness toward me. An unction came over me that I knew was from God. I grabbed his hand in a firm handshake and asked, "Can I pray for you?" He said, "Yes." I proceeded to pray something along these lines: "Father, bless my brother with direction, purpose and meaning in his life. Prosper him and give him success in all that he does. May your peace and blessing be upon him in every area of his life." I don't know if anything happened in his heart when I prayed those words, but I know something happened in mine. I was satisfied that I had done all that I could do to bring peace to the situation by offering prayer to the Father on his behalf and pronouncing a blessing upon him.

People won't always approve of who you are or what you do. The smallest thing can set a person against you without you even realizing it... and sometimes there's nothing you can do to "fix" it. But God showed me that night that I don't have to surrender in defeat to those situations. A word of prayer and blessing over the offended person lets them know that you're not against them, and it keeps you from becoming embittered toward them. It's been said thousands of times, but it's worthy of being repeated again... THERE IS POWER IN PRAYER!

Luke 6:28 (NIV)
Bless those who curse you, pray for those who mistreat you.

THE TEACHER IS A PUPIL
May 30 | November 27

About 10 years ago I attended a weekend Worship Music Conference in Florence, Alabama. Each attendee got to pick the classes he or she would attend during the weekend. I decided to go to a Songwriting Workshop for one of my class sessions. There was a young guy, about 25 years old, who was leading the class. About halfway through the class I looked over and saw Lenny LeBlanc sitting there, pen and paper in hand, taking notes. For those who don't know Lenny, he is a well-known singer/songwriter, and author of the Christian tunes "Above All" and "There is None Like You," not to mention the 70's Soft Rock Classic "Falling." I was stunned. I thought to myself, "Lenny should be teaching this class instead of this young guy."

When the class was over, I went over and talked with Lenny for a minute. I said to him "It blessed me to see you sitting in the seat of the Pupil when you could have just as easily been the Teacher." I don't remember his exact words, but he just smiled and replied with something like "There's always something you can learn from somebody else." Wow! What humility!

I've taken that moment with me these last several years, and have tried to keep that perspective as my own. If we are going to say "You're never too old to learn something new" then we also need to be willing to say "It doesn't matter who teaches me." Sometimes the OLDER needs to sit and learn from the YOUNGER, Sometimes the LEADER needs to sit and learn from the FOLLOWER…and sometimes the TEACHER needs to sit and learn from the PUPIL.

ANGRY PRAYERS

"Therefore I want the men everywhere to pray, lifting up holy hands without anger or disputing." 1 Timothy 2:8 (NIV)

"Without anger or disputing." Why did Paul add those stipulations at the end of this verse? Could it be that those are two things that hinder our prayers from being answered? Does God answer "angry prayers"? If He does, then why did Paul feel it was necessary to add the words "without anger or disputing"? There's a lot of anger in the world today, isn't there? Has that anger spilled over into your heart? Do you want your prayers to be answered? Consider getting the anger out of your heart.

PURGE
May 31 | November 28

When both of my children were first born I was pleased to find out that they had healthy hearts, lungs and bodies. After making sure all append-ages were present and accounted for, there was just one more tidbit of information that I waited on in order to feel confident that they were completely healthy... their first bowel movement. I know it's kind of a gross thought, and both of my kids would be mortified to find out I was writing about this, but when I saw their first bowel movement in their diapers, I was overjoyed! It was like stinky little piles of gold to me. Their digestive systems were fully functional and able to purge their bodies of all unwanted waste matter. That's important for newborn babies!

It's just a fact of life we've got to face... if your body can't properly purge out waste material you're highly susceptible to all kinds of diseases and sicknesses. Healthy bowels lead to a healthy body. Now, I know you're probably thinking, "What kind of spiritual application could this have?" I'm glad you asked.

In Matthew 15:17 Jesus said, "Whatever enters the mouth goes into the stomach and then out of the body." That's the way God set things up. Those who are sick, however, are not able to eliminate the waste products that go into their stomach. God made our bodies to be able to purge out all unnecessary waste products. There is a lesson for us spiritually in this.

Not everything that goes into our physical being (through our mouths) stays in our body... waste product is eliminated. The same is also true of our spiritual being. Things are coming into our spirit every day by way of words that we speak, or words that are spoken to us. I'll say it like this: Our ears are the mouths of our spirit... that's why Romans says "Faith comes by hearing." Those who have healthy spirits are able to purge out all the toxins and waste products that have entered their spirits through their ears. Not everything that enters our spirit should stay there. We need to learn to say "NO" to negative, harmful thoughts and words that try to attach to our spirit. We must eliminate them from our spirits if we want to be spiritually healthy. We must learn to PURGE ourselves.

2 Timothy 2:21 (KJV)
If a man therefore purge himself from these, he shall be a vessel unto honour, sanctified, and meet for the master's use.

THREE GENTS
June 1 | November 29

There are three "Gents" that you will meet
As you're traveling down life's street.

Three Gentlemen, with three different ways
Of finding success as they live out their days.

Intelli "Gent" is blessed with brains.
He knows stock markets and capital gains.

He has a very detailed plan for success...
He reads, he studies, then he invests.

Dili "Gent" has an interesting quirk,
He's willing to sweat, he knows how to work.

Just like Intelli, he has a plan for success...
He will give of his energy and he'll do his best.

Negli "Gent" won't think, work, or try.
He's completely content with "just getting by."

His plan for success? It seems rather silly...
He'll totally rely on Intelli and Dili.

Intelligent and Diligent, they have my respect,
But Negligent lives a life of neglect.

I will help Negli "Gent" all that I can,
But if he wants true success, he will need a new plan.

Proverbs 10:4 (NIV)
Lazy hands make for poverty, but diligent hands bring wealth.

Proverbs 21:5 (NAS)
The plans of the diligent lead surely to advantage,
But everyone who is hasty comes surely to poverty.

TAKING RESPONSIBILITY
June 2 | November 30

When I was in the 7th grade I tried out for the Jr. High Basketball team. didn't make the cut. So, when the next year of tryouts came I didn't eve attempt to try out for the team. I didn't try out for another school team fc the rest of my school years. When people asked me why I didn't try out fc the team I would say "Because of the politics involved... if the coaches don know you or like you they won't pick you." But, the truth of the matter wa I was intimidated by the "fear of rejection" that haunted me from my 7t grade year. I was also not willing to put in the time and effort to improv my basketball skills. So, I blamed others for my own deficiencies. Lots c people do that.

All of us are presented with opportunities for success, almost on a dail basis. Past rejections and lack of effort can keep us from realizing ou true potential. Looking back over my life up to this point, I realize tha I've not "fought" laziness in my life nearly enough. Taking the easy wa the least painful way, has often been my "mode of operation." I'm nc sure where I would be today if I would have broken through all my fear excuses, and laziness, but I'm sure I'd be better off. But it's not too late t start. It's not too late to change… to make adjustments… to reject rejec tion… to push through laziness and the "easy way." This next leg of m journey I am motivated to press onward. I will not dig myself into a rut. will not pursue comfort and ease. I will break through fears and timidit I will become the best ME I can be.

With this in mind, I've developed a simple equation for my own person: success. Here it is:

OPPORTUNITY + EFFORT - LAZINESS - EXCUSES = SUCCESS

Nobody has control over my own personal success but ME (with hel from God). Nobody can steal from my opportunities but ME. Nobod can be blamed for my deficiencies but ME. This is called TAKING RE SPONSIBILITY. I will RESPOND with the ABILITY that God has pu within me. I am determined… I WILL SUCCEED!

Philippians 4:13 (NAS)
I CAN do ALL THINGS through Christ who strengthens me.

"PAY" ATTENTION
June 3 | December 1

I had a very interesting dream one night about a man of God, whom I greatly respected, who passed away in 2004. Many of the details of the dream have become vague over the years but the most important part of the dream remains as crisp and sharp in my mind as the night I dreamed it. In the dream, this man of God was standing about 10 feet away from me. He turned in my direction, pointed his finger at me and said only two words, very authoritatively... PAY ATTENTION! I'll never forget that as long as I live. When I woke up from the dream I contemplated all that might have been meant by those words. Pay attention... to what? to whom? The dream presented as many questions as it did answers. But one thing is certain... it got my ATTENTION.

Take a close look at that two-word phrase... PAY ATTENTION. Notice the first word is PAY. Attention is like a currency. When you PAY ATTENTION you are making an investment. You're making a mental deposit. You are showing what you value in your life when you PAY attention to it. The problem most folks have with their attention is that they don't place the proper value on the things that should matter most, so they don't invest their attention properly. For example, paying more attention to a television show than to your spouse or child is a poor investment of your attention. Making too many unnecessary withdrawals from your attention resources will eventually leave you with a deficit. Attention deficit... that sounds familiar, doesn't it?!

Attention Deficit Disorder (A.D.D.) is a relatively new phenomenon in our modern society. Most think that the only cure for this disorder is medication. But, what if it's true that our attention is like currency? What if our attention can be strengthened and increased simply by placing the proper value on the things that matter most in life. How can this be done? The Bible gives a clear-cut solution when it says "My son, GIVE ATTENTION to my words; incline your ear to my sayings" (Proverbs 4:20). Those who place the proper value on God's Word and pay attention to what He says gain greater focus, and cannot be easily distracted. Yes, those who struggle with attention deficiencies would do well to spend time reading God's Word. His Word is just like medicine for our minds, for Proverbs 4:22 reminds us that God's words "are life unto those that find them and MEDICINE to all their flesh" (Jubilee Bible 2000).

WHO'S THAT WHISPERING IN MY EAR?
June 4 | December 2

I've often heard people ask the question, "How do you know when it's God talking to you, and not the devil?" I don't have all the answers, but here are a few things to consider when trying to distinguish who it is that's whispering in your ear.

1. God usually says "YOU CAN"... the devil usually says "YOU CAN'T!"
Person: Can I overcome this addiction?
God: You can!
Devil: You can't! You're not one of the lucky few who are able to overcome.

Philippians 4:13
"I CAN do all things through Christ who gives me strength."

2. When it comes to promises found in the Bible, God is saying "YES, you can have them"... the devil is saying "NO, you can't!"
Person: The Bible says I'm healed by the stripes on Jesus' back, but can I really be healed of my sickness?
God: YES, you can! My Word is true!
Devil: NO, you can't! You can't trust God or the Bible. You better have a back-up plan!

2 Corinthians 1:20
"For all the promises of God in Him are YES, and in Him AMEN."

3. God, most often times, is encouraging you with "DON'T BE AFRAID" ... the devil is telling you to "FEAR and WORRY!"
Person: I'm afraid I won't succeed in this new venture.
God: Don't be afraid. I am with you!
Devil: Be very afraid. You shouldn't even try this... it's too risky!

Mark 5:36 - "Do not be afraid; only believe."
Mark 6:50 - "Be of good cheer! It is I; do not be afraid."

Last thought: When God is speaking to us, His words are usually few. There's no reason for Him to explain, rationalize or negotiate with us. The devil, on the other hand, is known to be wordy in his approach with us. He will use rational arguments and human logic to distract us from what God has spoken to us. Remember Adam and Eve? Don't listen to him!

STAND
June 5 | December 3

I took my dog, Archie, to the dog park one morning so he could have some interaction with other dogs. On this particular morning there was a man there with two Great Danes. Archie had never seen a Great Dane before, so I thought it would be an interesting experiment to introduce him to the two giants.

All was going well as the three dogs did the typical dog-sniffing routine that all dog owners are accustomed to. The older male took a special interest in Archie and got a little too close to him. Archie felt threatened by the dog so he hunkered down a little bit, tucked his tail between his legs, and backed up. When he did that, the Great Dane growled at him and got in an attack posture. The dog's owner immediately restrained him and explained to me what had just happened. He said, "My dog is not an aggressive dog, but when he saw Archie getting in a retreat position, his Alpha male instincts kicked in because he sensed Archie's fear. He was trying to show his dominance." So, if Archie had just stood his ground, the Great Dane would have never gotten into an attack posture. When one dog backs down from another dog it taps into the dominant dog's aggressive instinct.

I learned a lot about dogs that morning as the other dog owner shared some of his dog-training insights and wisdom. I also got some extra insight into the spiritual battles that we humans face on a daily basis. You see, when a person is faced with adversity and feels extremely threatened, it is said that he has only two choices: FIGHT OR FLIGHT. Either the person will "put up his dukes" and fight, or he will "tuck tail and run." But, in Archie's situation, there was a third option available... STAND. Had Archie stood his ground there would have been no fight and no flight.

Listen. Our enemy, Satan, is a defeated foe. We have no reason at all to fear him. But, if he makes aggressive moves toward us, and we back down from him in retreat, we wind up allowing a defeated foe to dominate us. When he attacks we oftentimes feel threatened, and, yes, the "fight or flight" instinct within us begins to kick in. But, don't forget what Ephesians 6:13-14 reminds us to do in such cases: *"Having done all, to stand. STAND therefore...."*

1 Corinthians 16:13 (NLT)
Be on guard. STAND firm in the faith. Be courageous. Be strong.

PRAY FOR FAVOR
June 6 | December 4

I had just eaten lunch with a friend at a Chinese restaurant, and before we got up from the table to leave, my friend said, "Let me pray for you before we go." I'm always open to being prayed for, so I bowed my head and listened as my friend prayed. His prayer was short and sweet. He prayed, "Lord, bless Greg with Your favor today. In Jesus' name I pray. Amen." His prayer was not eloquent, lengthy or impressive by the world's standards, but it was greatly appreciated.

When we parted ways I decided I wanted a chocolate chip cookie for dessert, so I went to the bakery, just around the corner from where we had eaten lunch. I was greeted by friendly staff as I entered the doors. I saw one of their large, pre-packaged chocolate chip cookies, there on the shelf in front of me. I picked the cookie up and proceeded to the check-out counter. The clerk asked me what I wanted to order. I said, "I just wanted this cookie... that's it." The price on the giant cookie was $2.99. The clerk waved her hand at me as if to say, "Just take it." I was slightly confused and said, "I'm ready to pay for it," as I reached for my wallet. She wouldn't take my money... she gave me the cookie for free.

Now, I've been in that bakery on dozens of occasions before and that has never happened. But on this particular day, right after my friend prayed that I'd receive favor, I was given a free gift. When I got in my truck I called my friend and told him how quickly his prayer for me had been answered. Then I told him, "The next time you feel compelled to pray for God's favor on me, DO IT!"

As I drove home that day, I thought about how simple my friend's prayer was. His words were few, but the thing he asked for was specific... he prayed for FAVOR. I don't know why I haven't done the same thing for the people in my life, but now I am determined to be more intentional in my prayer for others.

MY PRAYER FOR TODAY:
"Lord, when I am with others remind me to pray for them, that Your favor will go with them, and that they will receive special blessings during their day so they will know how much You care for them."

Psalm 5:12 (NAS)
For it is You who blesses the righteous man, O LORD, You surround him with FAVOR as with a shield.

THE BEAUTY OF PURITY
June 7 | December 5

was eating lunch by myself at the Chick-fil-A restaurant in Decatur when I noticed a family standing in line, waiting to place their order. It was a husband and wife with two boys. The father, who was wearing his work uniform, was holding the younger boy in his arms. The boy looked to be three or four years old. It appeared that the father took his lunch break from work to spend time with his family.

knew nothing about the man. It was the first time I had ever seen him. But, as I watched the way his son responded to him I was blessed. As the father held the boy in his arms, the little boy would lean in to his father's chest, and look lovingly into his father's face as he talked with him. Then he did something that so captured my attention that it literally brought tears to my eyes. He reached his little hand to the back of his father's neck and caressed it. As the little boy talked to his father and mother he continued to caress the back of his father's neck. It was such an act of pure love that I wept as I watched.

The raw emotion I felt in that moment caught me by surprise. I found myself wiping tears from my eyes, hoping that nobody saw this grown man crying in a restaurant for no particular reason. Oh, but there was a reason... I was touched by purity.

The blessing continued as the little family sat down in a booth next to me. I tried not to be an eavesdropper, but I couldn't help but watch this family interact with one another. I suppose I was partly intrigued because of my own memory of my children when they were at that young, tender age. I so wanted to tell the mother and the father how their little family blessed me that day. I almost did it, but instead I just whispered a prayer over the young family, asking that the beauty and purity of the love that was shared would continue.

Purity is a beautiful thing to behold. Sometimes, when you're right in the middle of it, you're slightly blind to how sweet, holy and innocent it is. As time passes on, innocence and purity are challenged by the ugliness in the world around us. Look for purity every chance you get. When you feel it slipping away, seek after it desperately, for, Jesus reminds us in the Sermon on the Mount, "Blessed are the pure in heart, for they shall see God." I promise you... I SAW GOD that day in that little family, and that's why I was so blessed.

LOOSE LIPS
June 8 | December 6

Before I share the following thoughts I want to give a small disclaimer. have my own personal convictions about drinking alcoholic beverages but I don't impose my convictions upon others. Each person must have a persuasion within his own heart about his stance on drinking alcohol and it should be based on an understanding of God's Word, not the opinions and beliefs of others. Now, having said that let me share this thought for today.

Throughout the New Testament you will find several admonitions for the child of God to be "sober" and/or "sober-minded." In Paul's epistles to Timothy and Titus he states that one of the important qualifications for leaders in the church is that they be sober. Why is the word "sober" used I don't know all the reasons, but I have been around a few drunk people and a few "tipsy" people in my life. One thing I've noticed about people who've had a little too much to drink is that they have "loose lips." They say things that they wouldn't have said if they were sober. If you've been around drunk people, you know what I mean.

Sobriety keeps a person from saying things that they will later regret. Sobriety restrains a person from speaking harmful words to others. Those who are drunken throw caution to the wind and speak everything that's in their mind... many times to their own detriment.

Now, I am not making a statement about drinking alcohol, as I mentioned in my disclaimer above. What I want to emphasize is "loose lips." Christians need to be sober... they don't need to have "loose lips." They shouldn't say everything that comes into their head. Some things that come into our heads need to be restrained. But, if we're not sober-minded we'll let those words slip out. You can be a "Teetotaler" and still have loose lips. You can totally abstain from all alcoholic beverages and still not be sober-minded. God is calling us to put restraints on the words we speak. Those who want to be leaders in God's kingdom can't have loose lips... they must be SOBER.

1 Peter 5:8 (KJV)
Be sober, be vigilant; because your adversary the devil, as a roaring lion walketh about, seeking whom he may devour.

30 MINUTES A DAY
June 9 | December 7

When I was 14 years old, I began a discipline of lifting weights every day in hopes of becoming a body builder. If I had only kept up the discipline I had back then to work out 30 minutes a day, I would be a massive, muscular guy today... but I gave up!

When I was 16 years old, I started memorizing verses from the Bible daily. I had actually fully memorized the book of Romans with the exception of the 16th chapter. If I had only kept up the discipline I had back then to spend 30 minutes a day memorizing scriptures I would probably have the entire New Testament memorized by now... but I gave up!

About eight years ago I started each morning off by taking a 2 mile jog around my neighborhood. I did it to keep in shape and to build stamina. If I had only kept up the discipline to continue that 30 minute-a-day routine I would be in great shape today and could probably be running in a couple of 5K runs, and maybe even some half-marathons... but I gave up!

Isn't it interesting that a simple 30 minute-a-day discipline can have life-changing impact, if maintained on a daily basis? It is not the things that we "try to do" or the things we "hope to do" that have made us who we are today... it is the things that we consistently do in those 30 minute increments of our day. Simple disciplines in bite-sized portions – that's what makes us who we are. Challenge yourself today to start a new 30-minute-a-day routine to bring new discipline into your life.

MY PRAYER FOR TODAY:
"Lord, help me to better discipline my self to become all that I can be and all that You want me to be. In Jesus' name I pray. Amen."

1 Corinthians 9:24-27 (NAS)
Do you not know that those who run in a race all run, but only one receives the prize? Run in such a way that you may win. Everyone who competes in the games exercises self-control in all things. They then do it to receive a perishable wreath, but we an imperishable. Therefore I run in such a way, as not without aim; I box in such a way, as not beating the air; but I DISCIPLINE my body and make it my slave, so that, after I have preached to others, I myself will not be disqualified.

SEE THE CHILD INSIDE
June 10 | December 8

Several years ago, I was in a church service where prayer was requested for a child with a terminal illness. There was also an adult with a similar terminal disease that we were praying for during that service. When the service was over, an older lady in the church asked a question that has stuck with me since that day… "Why is it that we pray with more fervency for children who are facing adversity than for adults who are facing the same thing?" I suppose up to that moment in time I was not aware that I had been doing it, but when she said those words I realized that it was so.

We tend to have a greater heart of compassion for children than for adults. It is a part of our human nature. Millions of dollars worth of advertising are based upon this concept. Rarely do you see commercials showing adults begging for food in third world countries. No, you see the faces of innocent children. They pull on our heart strings and compel us to help. But, in just a few short years, that adorable little face of a child will be the rugged, less-adorable face of a young adult – less likely to pull compassion from our hearts. What is the solution to this dilemma? How can we maintain our compassion level for people even when they become adults?

I have found an answer, but it takes a little bit of imagination and creativity… TRY TO SEE THE CHILD INSIDE. I have done this on several occasions and it has brought me a greater sense of compassion for the adults I have dealt with and prayed for. Instead of seeing an adult standing in front of me asking for prayer, I've pictured them as the child that they once were years ago… perhaps running, laughing and playing on the playground. There is a reason why God's Word calls us "children of God." No matter how advanced we might get in years, God will always consider us to be His children. Oh, that we could see through His Eyes. Oh, that we could SEE THE CHILD INSIDE.

1 John 3:1-2 (NAS)
See how great a love the Father has bestowed on us, that we would be called CHILDREN of God; and such we are. For this reason the world does not know us, because it did not know Him. Beloved, now we are CHILDREN of God.

GET BETTER
June 11 | December 9

The good news of the Gospel is that God loves you "just the way you are." But, there's even better news than that… God can change you and make you "better than you are." Isn't that what we all want to be…BETTER? Sure, I'm content with who I am and with what I've been given, but I in no way want to stay where I am for the rest of my life. I want to reach higher. I want to achieve greater. I want to improve in every area of my life. Nobody who has a mind set on success wants to stay "just the way they are."

There truly is great comfort in knowing that God loves us just the way we are, with all of our faults, failures, and inconsistencies. But, His love does more than just accept us where we are… it takes us to a place where we become better. It takes us to a place where we're more like Him. It takes us to a place where He can use us BECAUSE OF who we are, instead of IN SPITE OF who we are.

Listen to this passage from The Message Bible, found in 2 Timothy 2:20-21: *"In a well-furnished kitchen there are not only crystal goblets and silver platters, but waste cans and compost buckets - some containers used to serve fine meals, others to take out the garbage. Become the kind of container God can use to present any and every kind of gift to his guests for their blessing."*

I'd be quite happy for God to use me as a garbage can in His kitchen. Just to be used for His service is an honor and a blessing. But, to be honest, I'd much rather be a silver platter or a crystal goblet that can be used to serve His guests at the dinner table. If I'm to progress from being a "garbage can" to a "silver platter," I'll need to get the garbage out of my life. I can't GET BETTER and BE BETTER if I continue to carry garbage with me everywhere I go!

MY PRAYER FOR TODAY:
Lord, I ask You to purge me and clean me from the impurities that prevent me from being used for noble use in Your kingdom. Show me the areas you want to work in my life to make me BETTER. I want to improve… I want to be more like You! In Jesus Name I pray, Amen.

THE "LITTLE TOE" IN CHRIST'S BODY
June 12 | December 10

Throughout my Christian walk I've heard sermons preached about the importance of the Body of Christ; how each member, no matter how insignificant they might feel, is truly important to the rest of the body. In response to that message, I used to laughingly say, "I'm so insignificant in Christ's Body, I'm probably just a LITTLE TOE!"

Well, recently, as I was watching a professional football game on TV, a commentator mentioned that the star running back for one of the teams was having to sit out of the game because of an injury. What crippling injury had he experienced that kept him from being on the field during that all-important game? He had sprained his LITTLE TOE. HaHa! Isn't that amazing? This professional athlete was dependent on his little toe to perform well on the playing field. As a matter of fact, he couldn't even stand firmly on his own two feet until the injured toe was healed.

So, there I was, saying, "I'm just a little toe in Christ's Body... I'm not that important," yet a highly-paid, professional athlete had to sit out of an important game because of an injury to his little toe!

Maybe you think you're unimportant in the grand scheme of things. You might think that the part you play in God's kingdom is insignificant. But, make no mistake... we all have a very important part to play in Christ's Body. Just a little revelation I received from a running back with an injured toe!

MY PRAYER FOR TODAY:
"Lord, use me in Your kingdom's work. Show me the important part I play in Your body. Maybe I am just a 'little toe' in Your body, but I know the Body of Christ needs me if it's going to STAND."

1 Corinthians 12:14-18 (NAS)
For the body is not one member, but many. If the foot says, "Because I am not a hand, I am not a part of the body," it is not for this reason any the less a part of the body. And if the ear says, "Because I am not an eye, I am not a part of the body," it is not for this reason any the less a part of the body. If the whole body were an eye, where would the hearing be? If the whole were hearing, where would the sense of smell be? But now God has placed the members, each one of them, in the body, just as He desired.

THE ANSWER IS "YES"
June 13 | December 11

sent some design work to one of my customers, and in my lengthy email to him I asked 4 specific questions. A few hours later I received a reply email. The email contained just one word... YES. I thought to myself, "Now what s he saying YES to? To which of my four questions does that word apply? looked back over the email I sent him and read my four questions again. It was then that I realized the answer was YES to all of the questions. Why say the same word four times when once is sufficient?! A smile came to my ace when I realized the clever way my customer had responded to all of my questions. He wasn't being rude, or short with me... he was just being uccinct and to the point.

My customer's response reminded me of one of my favorite scripture verses: "For all the promises of God in him are YES, and in him Amen, to the glory of God by us." (2 Corinthians 1:20 - American King James Version). Ask God any question you want to about His love, care and forgiveness or you... I can guarantee you what His response will be. "Does God love me? Does God forgive me? Does God want to heal me? Does God want to bless me?" Just one word answers all of those questions... YES!

DON'T TAKE PEACE FOR GRANTED

Within the space of three weeks we had two new families move in to our neighborhood. One afternoon, the neighbors who moved in across the street asked me, "Is it always this quiet in this neighborhood?" I hadn't really thought about our neighborhood as being quiet, but they had moved in from a very busy, noisy neighborhood and were taken aback by the quietness. I said, "Yes, I guess it is a very peaceful neighborhood."

told my wife about the conversation I had with the new neighbors across the street and she said, "The new neighbors behind us asked me the exact same question! "Is it always this quiet in this neighborhood?"

To be honest, neither I nor my wife had given much thought to the peacefulness of our neighborhood until our new neighbors made us aware of it. Likewise, the Christian often takes for granted the peace they so frequently enjoy without realizing what a blessing it is. Do you realize the importance of the peace you carry with you? Do you know that those who don't know Christ don't have that peace? Don't take it for granted!

FORGET WHAT'S BEHIND YOU

June 14 | December 12

Lately, I've been having difficulty remembering things that have happened in my past. Now, you might think I would be a little alarmed about this forgetfulness, but actually, I see it as a good thing. No, I'm not suffering from dementia or senility. I've just been reading Philippians 3:13 which says, "FORGETTING those things which are behind, and reaching for those things which are before."

You see, FORGETTING things from the past (both good and bad) can be very healthy for us as we press on toward our future. Sure, everybody wants to put the "bad stuff" from the past out of their memory banks. The bad memories can sadden and depress us. But sometimes even the good memories can hinder us on our journey... they can keep us from "looking forward" because, just like Lot's wife, we're always looking back at how things "used to be."

You remember Lot's wife, don't you? Interestingly enough, one of the shortest verses in the Bible refers to Lot's wife. In Luke 17:32, Jesus said, "Remember Lot's wife!" Why did he tell us to remember her? Because she is symbolic of those who look back on the past longingly and affectionately instead of looking ahead to the place where God is leading us. She was told by the angels of God not to look back, but she disobeyed. You've heard the rest of the story. When she looked back she became "the pillar of the family." (Pun intended)

God is telling us today the same thing He told Lot and his family several thousand years ago... "DON'T LOOK BACK." Forget what's behind you.

Yes, I've been kind of forgetful these days...I suggest you give it a try.

Philippians 3:13 (NLT)
No, dear brothers and sisters, I have not achieved it, but I focus on this one thing: Forgetting the past and looking forward to what lies ahead.

Genesis 19:17, 26 (KJV)
Escape for thy life; LOOK NOT BEHIND THEE... But his wife looked back from behind him, and she became a pillar of salt.

STAY CLOSE!
June 15 | December 13

I had taken my dog, Archie, along with me on one of my morning walks. Now, Archie is sort of a hyperactive dog, so he's always pulling on his leash, wanting to get where we're going as fast as possible. I tugged on the leash several times to get him to slow down. There was a time or two that he pulled so hard it felt like he could rip my arm out of socket. I got aggravated with him and reprimanded him several times as we walked along. When we finally got back to my house I mused about how Archie's relationship with me is much like my relationship with the Lord. Yes, sometimes I get a little too anxious and try to "get out ahead" of God... that's when God gives me a gentle pull to reel me back to His side.

I wrote this little poem as a fun way of keeping a proper perspective on my relationship with "My Master."

Are you walking me, or am I walking you?
Sometimes it's hard to tell Who's walking Who!

When I put on your leash You set off like a rocket
And you almost pull My arm out of socket!

I want you to learn that I am the Leader…
I am the Master and you are the Heeder.

When you pull ahead and jerk on the leash
You're choking yourself and you get out-of-reach.

So I pull you back and bring you close to me.
One day you will learn that's the best place to be.

As I speak these words to my dog, as his master,
God speaks them to me as my loving Pastor.

He tells me "Stay Close, don't pull out ahead,
Let Me be your Leader. Obey what I've said."

Then he brings me back with His gentle pull,
And I walk beside him... there my heart is FULL!

TURN IT AROUND
June 16 | December 14

Several years ago, on a chilly Spring morning, I started out on my morning walk, wearing just a flimsy hooded jacket. The farther I walked along the more I realized that I wasn't dressed warmly enough. Halfway through my walk I found shelter from the cutting wind beneath some large pine trees. I sat there with my hood pulled over my head, and prayed for God's guidance for the day ahead.

As I sat there praying and meditating a police car drove up a few dozen feet away from me. I didn't think much about it at first, until I noticed that the police officer was walking towards me. Sure enough, he walked straight up to me and said, "Sir, there's been a complaint about you sitting here. You look rather suspicious. What are you doing here?" I said, "Are you kidding me?" He replied, "No, I'm not. What are you doing here?" I sort of laughed and said, "Actually, I was sitting here praying." The officer replied, "That's nice... do you have any identification on you?" I never carry any ID with me on my morning walks, so I replied, "No."

Just then I noticed another police officer come up behind me. Two officers had been called to "apprehend" me (the dangerous criminal that I am). The place began to look like a legitimate crime scene! Because I was wearing the hooded jacket I suppose I looked like a gangster or something. I told the two officers that I lived just down the road. One of the officers followed me home in his car to verify that I was telling the truth.

Later that week, as I told many of my friends and acquaintances what had happened to me, they wondered why I laughed as I told the story. Some said, "That would have made me so mad to get treated that way." I guess I just look at things differently. That was the most exciting thing that had happened to me in months. The idea of me being looked upon as some kind of criminal was rather amusing to me. I really got a kick out of it.

This leads me to my thought for today. Do you know how to put a positive spin on a seemingly negative situation? You don't necessarily have to laugh about it, or find humor in it, but can you imagine, just for a minute, that God can take your negative situation and turn it around? God has promised that He makes everything that happens in our lives turn out for good. Do you believe that? If so, why are you getting so uptight about the negative circumstances you find yourself in? Find the good... TURN IT AROUND.

NOT WITH THAT MOUTH!
June 17 | December 15

I let my dog, Archie, sit in my lap for a couple of minutes one morning before I started my workday at the computer. He was about nine months old at the time. He hadn't sat in my lap since he was a little puppy so he was enjoying the attention I was giving him. In appreciation for the love I was showing, he reached up and gave me a big slobbery kiss on my mouth when I wasn't looking. Part of me said "Yuck!" while the other part of me enjoyed the tender moment.

The tenderness of that moment, however, was overshadowed the next morning when I caught sight of Archie eating cat poo in my backyard. It almost made me sick to my stomach, just thinking I let that nasty mouth give me a big slobbery kiss the day before. I called Archie to me, looked him in the face and said, "It'll be a long time before I let you give me another kiss on my mouth!" Now, I've heard people say, "A dog's mouth is much cleaner and sterile than a human's mouth." Even if that is remotely true about other dogs, I know it couldn't be true about my cat poo-eating dog! He eventually grew out of that bad habit, thankfully.

This leads me to my thought for today. I will confess that I don't have the "cleanest" mouth on this planet. There are times that I've let curse words slip out during a moment of frustration or anger. I'm ashamed of myself when that happens and I try to quickly ask God for forgiveness when it does happen. Why? Because this is the same mouth that I BLESS God with. It just doesn't seem right to let cursing and swearing come from my mouth one moment, then words of praise and adoration to my God come out the next moment. I wonder, when we do that, if God has the same reaction that I had when I saw Archie eating cat poo?

When I was growing up, if a person released a string of curse words from their mouth, there were those who would humorously reply with, "Do you kiss your mother with that mouth?!" I'll ask a similar question… "Do you praise your God with that mouth?!"

James 3:10 (KJV)
Out of the same mouth proceedeth blessing and cursing. My brethren, these things ought not to be so.

FOOLISH PRAYERS
June 18 | December 16

One of the eighth grade boys in my Wednesday night discipleship group asked if he could lead in prayer one night. Of course, I was ecstatic that he was so zealous to pray so I granted his request. The prayer he offered up put a grin on my face. He prayed, "Lord, save everyone in the world, and heal everyone who is sick." Those were the simple, heart-felt words that poured from this young man's heart. The reason I grinned? I remember praying that exact same prayer when I was his age. That was back when I was "young and naive."

I'm older now, and I've been around long enough to know that those kinds of prayers don't get answered. After all, there's no way God can save EVERYONE in the world, and He can't heal EVERYONE who is sick... that's IMPOSSIBLE! Gosh, did I just say something was IMPOSSIBLE for God?! Could it be that I've become so "spiritually mature" that I no longer believe God can do impossible things? I might have prayed prayers like that when I was young and naive but I'm much too logical and rational in my thinking to pray like that today. Yes, I'm refined, educated and mature.

When the boy's prayer ended, I considered taking a moment to bring a little correction to his choice of words in prayer. I almost broke out into a theological dissertation on why God can't save "everybody" in the world because He would have to override their free will in order to do it. I almost explained to Him that not everyone who is sick has faith to be healed by God, so it would be an impossibility for God to answer that prayer. Yes, I almost took him aside to "set him straight." I felt it my duty as a "mature Christian."

The more I thought about it, however, the more I realized I needed HIM to set ME straight. His prayer unearthed a buried and forgotten zeal for God that I once had. There was a time when I prayed prayers like that. But it seems like the "smarter" I've gotten the less I've prayed those impossible, "foolish" prayers. Lord revive the child-like faith I once had, when I truly thought that NOTHING WAS TOO HARD FOR YOU."

Jeremiah 32:17 (NAS)
Ah Lord GOD! Behold, You have made the heavens and the earth by Your great power and by Your outstretched arm! Nothing is too difficult for You.

SHOUT!
June 19 | December 17

.t was a rainy November morning when I was on my morning walk with God. It was a Friday morning, to be exact. Now, on Fridays, I have a specific plan of action during my morning walks. Many years ago I felt like I was instructed by the Lord to make my Friday morning walks a time of worship and praise. So I try my best not to "ask" for anything in prayer... no petitions, no supplications, no intercessions... just simple words of praise and adoration lifted up to my loving, Heavenly Father. We would all do well to set aside some time during our week just for praise and worship, outside of our regular church services. He deserves it, Amen?

So, there I was, walking along, praising God and lifting words of worship and adoration to Him, when I heard the distant sound of an approaching train. I was walking down a road that was just 20 yards away from the railroad tracks. As the train got closer I could hear the roaring engine getting louder and louder. The closer it got, the more it was drowning out my voice of praise to God. What did I do? I lifted my voice louder and louder to compensate for the approaching engine's noise. Finally, the train's engine was right beside me and the noise from the engine overpowered my voice to the point I couldn't even hear what I was saying.

When the engine passed by, that's when this revelation came to me... "That's why you've got to SHOUT TO THE LORD!" No, God's not deaf or hard of hearing, but there is so much noise in this world that tries to drown out the praise and worship that God deserves, so the people of God must be purposeful in their attempts to block out all the interruptions and distracting noises that are out there. When the world is being extremely noisy and loud, we can do one of two things: 1) Let the noise overpower us and distract us, or 2) Get louder.

Sometimes you've just got to shout! Your voice of praise to God has to be louder than the distracting noise of this world. God is deserving of praise and you know it's true, so when this world is trying to drown out your praise and worship to God, be determined in your heart to be louder than the noise. LIFT UP A SHOUT!

Psalm 98:4 (NLT)
Shout to the LORD, all the earth; break out in praise and sing for joy!

MAKE YOUR OWN GATES
June 20 | December 18

Many think it strange when I tell them that my morning walks with God take place at the local cemetery. You see, the Hartselle Cemetery is just two blocks from my house... just a short five minute walk away. Once I enter the cemetery it's like I'm in a quiet, peaceful sanctuary, secluded from the rest of the world. It's the perfect place to spend quiet time praying and seeking God, and also taking in the beauty of nature that surrounds the cemetery.

A fence once surrounded the cemetery, and there was a beautiful entrance way, complete with an ornate gate and surrounding trees, shrubbery and flowering plants that greeted all who entered the gates. Recently, however, the city of Hartselle removed the fence and the entrance gate with plans to erect a new, more ornate fence and entrance way in the future. For years, as I entered the old gated entrance way it felt like I was "entering into" my own secluded haven... getting away from the world so I could spend time with my Maker. I would often quote the verse from Psalm 100, "I will enter His GATES with thanksgiving" as I entered through the gates to the cemetery. It was a great visual for me to grab hold of.

Now, those gates are gone. The trees, shrubs and flowering plants are gone, too. There is currently nothing there at the entrance way to welcome those who enter the cemetery. There's just a flat asphalt road.

The first day I entered the cemetery after the demolition of the old gated entrance way I felt like I had lost a dear old friend. I complained to the Lord, "There are no gates for me to enter through into Your presence." In my heart I heard these words, "Make your own gates!" Now, doesn't that sound just like something the Lord would say? So, I began to visualize the old gateway that once stood there and imagined myself passing through the gates. I then repeated the scripture, "I will enter His gates with thanksgiving." I made my own entryway into God's presence by getting a vision of the gates that were once there.

This is the power that we all have... the creative ability to visualize a personal entrance way into God's presence, no matter what situation we are in. Whether we are in a remote desert, on a mountaintop, or in the heart of a concrete jungle, we can make our very own entrance way into God's presence, just by visualizing it in our hearts, and repeating the verse, "I will enter HIS GATES with thanksgiving!"

LORD, TEACH ME
June 21 | December 19

LORD TEACH ME...

Teach me how to minister Your healing touch to those who are sick,
But also teach me how to minister compassion to those who do not
receive healing.

Teach me how to proclaim truth to those who have never been taught,
But also teach me how to be merciful to those who hold on to lies and
refuse to listen to the truth.

Teach me how to gain wealth and to manage my finances properly,
But also teach me how to be content with what I have and to trust in Your
faithfulness when it seems like wealth is elusive.

Teach me how to be strong emotionally and spiritually,
But also teach me about the power You make available to those who
are weak, for You said that Your strength is made perfect in weakness.

Teach me how to be bold in approaching Your throne of Grace,
But also teach me how to bow in humble adoration before You.

Teach me how to always believe the best in other people,
But also teach me how to be forgiving when others let me down.

Teach me how to succeed in every area of my life,
But also teach me how to remain humble no matter what success I
might achieve.

Teach me how to care for others with heart-felt intensity,
But also teach me how to cast all my cares on You, for You care for me.

Teach me how to stand up for what I believe and fight for what is right,
But also teach me how to choose my battles carefully.

I still have so much to learn, Lord. I can't teach others until I have first
been taught by You.

LORD TEACH ME.

MY HEAD'S STUCK IN THE CLOUDS
June 22 | December 20

I've had some people tell me
"Your head's stuck in the clouds!"
Those words were meant to shame me
Instead, they made me proud.

"Set your mind on things above"
That's what's written in God's Word,
So, when my head's stuck in the clouds
I'm just obeying what I've heard.

When my head's not in the clouds
It's stuck on things down here.
It's set on things of Earth
Where there's hopelessness and fear.

I do this Earth no good
If I have no hope or love,
So, my head's stuck in the clouds,
I set my mind on things above.

Colossians 3:2 (NAS)
Set your mind on the things above, not on the things that are on earth.

GOD IS PRESENT TENSE!

He's the God of NOW,
Not just the God of THEN.
He's the God who IS,
Not the God who's BEEN.
He's the God who DID,
But still the God who DOES.
He's the Great I AM…
Not the Great I WAS!

Exodus 3:14 (KJV)
Thus shalt thou say unto the children of Israel,
I AM hath sent me unto you.

WE WIN!
June 23 | December 21

I've heard people say (referring to the Bible) "I've read the back of the book... and we win!" While that statement is true, I'd also like to say, "I've read the beginning of the book, one-quarter of the way through the book, halfway through the book, five-eighths of the way through the book, three-quarters of the way through the book, and seven-eighths of the way through the book... and we win!"

Check this out:

BEGINNING OF THE BOOK:
"In your unfailing love you will lead the people you have redeemed. In your strength you will guide them to your holy dwelling.. The nations will hear and tremble." - Exodus 15:13-14 (NIV)

ONE QUARTER OF THE WAY THROUGH THE BOOK:
"No one will be able to stand against you all the days of your life. As I was with Moses, so I will be with you; I will never leave you nor forsake you." - Joshua 1:5 (NIV)

HALFWAY THROUGH THE BOOK:
"My God in His lovingkindness will meet me; God will let me look triumphantly upon my foes" - Psalm 59:10 (New American Standard 1977)

FIVE-EIGHTHS OF THE WAY THROUGH THE BOOK:
"No weapon that is formed against you shall prosper" - Isaiah 54:17 (NAS)

THREE QUARTERS OF THE WAY THROUGH THE BOOK:
"But the people that do know their God shall be strong, and do exploits" Daniel 11:32 (KJV)

SEVEN-EIGHTHS OF THE WAY THROUGH THE BOOK:
"In all these things we are more than conquerors through him who loved us" - Romans 8:37 (NIV)

BACK OF THE BOOK:
"And they overcame him because of the blood of the Lamb and because of the word of their testimony" Revelation 12:11 (NAS)

STANDING IN THE GAP
June 24 | December 22

I was driving down Main Street on my way home from church one Sunday morning and took a right turn on Milner Street. As I turned onto Milner Street I noticed, right there at the intersection of Main Street and Milner Street, a big batch of roofing nails scattered all over the road. There were over 100 assorted sizes and shapes of nails, just sitting there, waiting to pierce through the tires of oncoming cars. Many of the nails were actually in the middle of Main Street, and passersby were running over them, not knowing what they were until it was too late.

I was initially going to drive on by and let someone else take care of the problem, but a sense of responsibility came over me. I pulled over and got out of my truck to clean up the mess. It took about five minutes to get all the nails up. Cars were lining up at the stop sign at Milner to merge onto Main Street. Some cars beeped their horns at me. I tried to explain the reason why I was blocking traffic... hopefully saving motorists from getting punctured tires. I've had to pay for two tire punctures in the last two years, so I was acting out of empathy for my fellow man. Did those who were irritated by the blockage in the traffic flow understand what I was doing, or appreciate my actions? I'm not sure. But I do know that I probably prevented a half-dozen motorists from getting flat tires that morning.

When you think about it, that's what we Christians are called to do. We're called to tell the world that there's impending danger ahead for those who continue down the wrong road. We're called to stop the flow of everyday traffic just long enough to plant a seed of warning in the lives of those who aren't aware of the consequences for going down that wrong road. We're called to "stand in the gap" between people and their eternal destiny... to make an eternal difference in people's lives. As I was cleaning up the nails in the road that day I saw at least three cars make a U-turn to avoid the intersection I was standing in. Though I know they were irritated by the detour, I also know that they were saved from the certain harm that would have come to them that morning if I hadn't been STANDING IN THE GAP.

Ezekiel 22:30 (NAS)
I searched for a man among them who would build up the wall and stand in the gap before Me for the land, so that I would not destroy it; but I found no one.

I'M NOT A HUMAN BEING!
June 25 | December 23

When my daughter was three years old, she and I were sitting in our backyard feeding bread crumbs to some sparrows. She was sitting in my lap. I told her she needed to be very quiet and still so as not to startle the birds and scare them off. She giggled as the tiny birds hopped closer toward us, getting braver and braver with every morsel that we tossed their way. As we threw the crumbs toward them we encouraged them to come even closer to us by saying, "Here birds, come here birdie birds." The closer they got, the more excited she got. Finally, the excitement got too much for her, so she jumped up out of my lap, stood to her feet and exclaimed, "Here, birdie birds!" Her sudden movement startled the birds and they flew off, thus ending our creature encounter for the day. When the birds flew off, my daughter asked, "Daddy, why did the birds fly away?" I replied, "Because they're afraid of human beings." My daughter quickly replied, "But I'm not a human being... I'm just a little girl!" Oh, the innocence. It brought a smile to my face. I still call her "little girl" to this day.

Sixteen years later, my daughter and I watched the television as horrifying news came from Sandy Hook Elementary School in Newton, Connecticut. A gunman entered the school and shot and killed 20 school children. I looked over at my daughter and saw tears of disbelief streaming down her face. The reality of what "human beings" were capable of doing was all too real to my "little girl" at that moment.

When it was time to send my daughter off to college, I wondered if I had prepared her enough for all that was out there in the world. I was about to send my "little girl" out into a world filled with "human beings." It was a sobering moment for me. It brought new meaning to what Jesus said to His disciples just before He sent them out to preach the gospel. He said, "Go, I am sending you out like lambs among the wolves" (Luke 3:10).

Child of God, you are innocent and pure, made clean by the blood of Jesus. Yet, Father God calls you to go out into this world filled with "human beings" so you can be an agent of change... to bring light and purity to a world filled with darkness and evil. You have been commissioned by Jesus to go out like "lambs among the wolves." May the purity and innocence you possess be a beacon that points many to our loving Father in Heaven. May you bring other "children" into the Father's family today!

FACE YOUR FEAR
June 26 | December 24

I awoke before sunrise to take my morning walk on a cold October morn
ing. When I checked the weather I found out that it was 37° outside, so
put on a thick jacket and began to look for my gloves. I couldn't find them
in any of the usual places. I remembered taking them with me the day be
fore on my morning walk, but I couldn't remember where I put them after
returning home. After five minutes I gave up the search and headed out the
back door. I decided my hands would just have to be cold that morning.

It was still dark outside as I walked on my usual course to the local
cemetery where I take my morning walk. Normally I cut through on a
gravel road as a short-cut to the cemetery, but I noticed that there was
a car parked in the middle of the gravel road this particular morning. It
looked very suspicious to me. Just to be honest the idea of walking up to
a parked car on a gravel road in the dark kind of spooked me. When
felt that fear rise up inside me, I decided to avoid the shortcut and take
the long way to the cemetery, down the well-lit sidewalk. I walked along
about 50 yards when I was suddenly overwhelmed by the conviction of
the Holy Spirit. Within myself I heard a voice of exhortation, "Why are
you afraid? The Greater One is inside you." I quoted the verse, "The Lord
is my Light and my Salvation, whom shall I fear" (Psalm 27:1), then
back-tracked to the gravel road short-cut to face my own fears.

As I walked along and got closer to the parked car I gained greater con
fidence that I was safe and there was no need to be afraid. Then some
thing interesting happened. In the darkness I saw something black on
the gravel road ahead of me. I turned the flashlight feature of my iPhone
on, and there they were... the gloves that I had been frantically searching
for earlier. They must have fallen out of my pockets on my walk the day
before. A smile came to my face as I realized why the Spirit of God gave
me courage that morning. He gave me courage to face my fears so I could
find something that I had lost.

Just think... if I had obeyed the voice of fear that morning I wouldn't have
found my gloves. But, because I listened to the voice of the Spirit (the
voice of courage), that which was lost was restored to me. So remember...
disobey the voice of fear every chance you get. It's trying to make you
miss out on the blessing that God has for you!

SHANIQUA
June 27 | December 25

I was sitting on the front row at church as the pastor was sharing an interesting testimony that a friend of his told him. This particular friend was not yet a believer in Jesus Christ when this story took place, but later surrendered His heart to the Lord.

The man was walking on the beach with his wife and two kids (who were believers) and from out of nowhere, and for no particular reason, the word "Shaniqua" came out of his mouth. He thought it was strange that he had said that word and wondered why that happened. As they walked along the beach further they saw some teenagers drawing something in the sand on the beach ahead of them. When they got to the place where the teenagers were he noticed that they had written a gigantic word in the sand... the word was SHANIQUA. The man thought it was some kind of strange coincidence and commented on it to his wife and kids.

Later, as he was talking on the phone to my pastor about the incident, he asked him if it was just some kind of strange coincidence. The pastor said, "It's obvious that God is trying to get your attention and He used this random word SHANIQUA to reach out to you. This was not a coincidence at all. God is showing you that there are things outside your logical, rational thinking that He wants to convey to you."

As I listened to this story I wasn't totally satisfied that the word SHANIQUA was just a random word God used to get this man's attention. I decided to Google the name SHANIQUA on my iPhone to see if it was just a random name, or if it had a special meaning behind it. A chill went down my spine as I read that Shaniqua is a derivative of the African name Shanika, which means GOD IS GRACIOUS. God was speaking to this unbeliever's heart and telling him, "I am Gracious."

Later that morning, I told the pastor what I had discovered about the meaning of the name SHANIQUA. He was awed by the fact that God used that particular word to speak to his friend. I asked him, "Are you going to tell your friend what Shaniqua means?" He replied, "Are you kidding me? Absolutely!"

God is Gracious... and He will use some interesting methods to get that message over to us!

I WILL DIRECT MY PRAYER
June 28 | December 26

Psalm 5:3 (KJV)
My voice shalt thou hear in the morning, O LORD; in the morning will I
DIRECT MY PRAYER unto thee, and will look up.

I was thinking about the above verse on one of my morning walks when the words "I direct my prayer unto thee" captured my attention. I thought within myself, "Why does that verse tell us to 'direct' our prayer to God? Isn't all prayer directed toward God? Is there somewhere else (or someone else) other than God, that prayers can be directed to?" There must be... otherwise why would this verse specifically mention directing prayers to God?

It helps to first understand what the word PRAY means. In it's simplest form, PRAY means "to make a request." In the scriptures, particularly in the Old Testament, you will find that the word PRAY is interchangeable with the word ASK or REQUEST. For instance, when Abraham went to Egypt with his wife Sarah (Genesis 12:13), he made a request of her. He said, "Say, I pray thee, thou art my sister, that it may be well with me for thy sake" (Notice how the word "pray" is used in this verse.) He did not ask for God to help him... he asked Sarah to help him. The scriptures are full of such verses where one person makes a request of another person by saying "I pray thee." In such cases, it could be said that people were directing their prayers to other people... not to God. Unfortunately, we do this all the time. We ask others to fill a need in our lives that only God is supposed to fill.

So, I'm challenged by this thought today. Am I directing my prayers (my requests) to God, or to other people? Am I requesting medical science and doctors to heal me of my sickness? Am I requesting government to meet my financial needs? Am I requesting friends to fill the loneliness inside my soul? Am I requesting my pastor to give me direction in my spiritual life? Where does my help come from? From God... or from people? If my help comes from God, then my prayers (requests) should be directed to Him.

Philippians 4:6 (NAS)
Be anxious for nothing, but in everything by prayer and supplication
with thanksgiving let your REQUESTS be made known to God.

SING... AND FEEL BETTER

June 29 | December 27

"Come before His presence with SINGING." - Psalms 100:2 (KJV)

God has requested that those who come before Him do so with SINGING. For some reason God is blessed by the sounds of our voices lifted to Him in SONG. But, He is not the only one Who gets BLESSED when we sing to Him! A recent medical study suggests that singing is powerful medicine to the person who does it frequently. The following is an excerpt from an article on TIME.COM about the effects of singing:

> "The elation may come from endorphins, a hormone released by singing, which is associated with feelings of pleasure. Or it might be from oxytocin, another hormone released during singing, which has been found to alleviate anxiety and stress. Oxytocin also enhances feelings of trust and bonding, which may explain why still more studies have found that singing lessens feelings of depression and loneliness."

Isn't it interesting that God requests us to come before Him with a song upon our lips? He knows what medical science is just now finding out... SINGING is a powerful medicine for our souls. So, if you're down, depressed or feeling lonely, try something a little different today to overcome those feelings... Come into God's presence WITH A SONG!

Psalm 95:2 (NAS)
Let us come before His presence with thanksgiving, Let us shout joyfully to Him with psalms.

Psalm 81:1 (KJV)
Sing aloud unto God our strength: make a joyful noise unto the God of Jacob.

Colossians 3:16 (NAS)
Let the word of Christ richly dwell within you, with all wisdom teaching and admonishing one another with psalms and hymns and spiritual songs, SINGING with thankfulness in your hearts to God.

KEEP HOLDING ON!
June 30 | December 28

I conducted an object lesson for a large group of Elementary kids at church a few years ago. I was trying to teach them the meaning of the word ENDURANCE. In Matthew 24:13 Jesus said, "He who endures to the end will be saved" so knowing what the word ENDURE means would put the kids at a definite advantage.

I set up a platform with a bar hanging across two wooden poles in the center of the room. A rope was suspended from the bar. I then asked for a volunteer from the audience. A little third-grade girl raised her hand and I called her forward. I asked the little girl to grab hold of the rope as I lifted her up about two feet off the ground. She grasped the rope in her hands, I released her. She hung there, clinging to the rope, her feet about two feet above ground. As she clung to the rope I told her and the class "Endurance is when you hang on as long as you can…and then you keep on hanging on."

I asked the little girl to let me know when she was getting tired of holding on to the rope. About a minute later she said she was getting tired. The rest of the class cheered her on. I told her "Just promise me you won't let go and drop to the floor until you've first let me know that you've hung on as long as you can." A few moments later she said "I'm about to drop, I can't hold on any longer." Right when she said that I had a couple of assistants quickly come into the room and put a large tub of water just beneath her feet. If she released her grip from the rope she would fall into the water and get soaked. She let out a little scream as she gripped the rope more tightly and pulled herself up from the water below, and the class full of kids got a good laugh in the process. The little girl suddenly discovered that she could hold on longer than she originally thought. She gained a new appreciation for the word ENDURANCE that day.

So, I leave you with this word of encouragement today: HOLD ON….. and when you think you've held on as long as you can, KEEP HOLDING ON. There is a prize waiting for those who ENDURE, for those who remain strong and won't quit. HOLD ON FOR THE PRIZE!

Philippians 3:14 (NAS)
I press on toward the goal for the prize of the upward call of God in Christ Jesus.

CHEERS!
December 29

My family and I were sitting around the dinner table on Christmas Eve, about to partake of the feast my wife had prepared. In appreciation for all of my wife's hard work, I stood and raised my glass of ice water in a toast to honor her. Those around the table all lifted their own glass of beverage… some had ice water, some sweet tea, and some a glass of wine. As we clinked our glasses together my wife questioned the proper etiquette for making a toast. "Can you make a toast when everyone's glasses aren't filled with the same drink?" she asked. I'm certainly not the one to answer questions on proper etiquette in such situations, but after a pause I responded with my own heart-felt understanding… "Well, of course you can! That's the beauty of it. It's diversity coming together in unity to bring honor to the one being toasted!"

Revelation comes to us in some beautiful ways. That moment gave me an even greater appreciation for what would happen Christmas morning at my home church.

As I stood upon the stage leading worship Christmas morning I looked out across the congregation. Such diversity was contained in our small gathering. We were not all of the same age range, not of the same upbringing, not of the same ethnicity, not of the same denominational background… yet we were all gathered around a unifying thought and appreciation for the Savior who was born into the world on the very first Christmas morning. We "raised our glasses" filled with praise and adoration for our Savior and Lord and toasted Him, even though our own cup of life was not filled with the same experiences or background. He was honored by our diversity coming together in unity to bring Him worship.

Yes, it's a sad reality of life… our diversity most often-times divides and separates us from one another. But, when our diversity comes together around the central theme of Jesus Christ, He is honored and we see our walls of division slowly disintegrate. Truly, Jesus came to bring "Peace on Earth, Good will to men."

Ephesians 2:14 (NAS)
For He Himself is our peace, who made both groups into one and broke down the barrier of the dividing wall.

TENACITY
December 30

On my walk one morning in early January, I saw one lone leaf clinging tightly to the barren branch of a very large oak tree. All the other leaves of that tree (every single one) had fallen several weeks earlier, but that one tenacious little leaf just kept holding on to life. It was a moment of inspiration for me. It not only captured my attention... it spoke to my spirit. It was the perfect illustration and definition of the word TENACITY... a character trait that I sometimes lack in my life.

Here's the dictionary definition of the word TENACITY:
The quality or fact of being able to grip something firmly.

Do you have TENACITY? Are you able to hold on tightly and firmly to the things that you believe, and the things that are most important in this life? Or, when things get difficult, do you tend to take the path of least resistance, and just give up and succumb to the struggle? Can you hold on tightly to your beliefs and convictions even though everyone else around you has surrendered theirs to be accepted by this world? It's easy to hold on to your convictions when you have the support of others around you, but what about when you're all alone, and there's no one to cheer you on?

Now, eventually, that one tenacious leaf was going to fall to the ground and become compost. It would be naive of me to think otherwise. But just for that moment in time, it remained on the tree, clinging to its source of life, not concerned that it stood alone... not concerned that all others had released their grip. In doing so, it spoke to me and motivated me to hang on even more tightly to my life source, my Heavenly Father, even when I see others around me letting go. I am determined to be more tenacious than ever. I am determined... I'll not release my grip!

John 15:5 (KJV)
I am the vine. You are the branches. He who remains in me, and I in him, the same bears much fruit, for apart from me you can do nothing.'

Colossians 1:11 (NIV)
Being strengthened with all power according to his glorious might so that you may have great endurance and patience.

SWING THE BAT
December 31

My dad was a consummate athlete. When I was growing up we had a trophy case that displayed all of my dad's trophies. He had won trophies in every sport imaginable. He had volleyball trophies, basketball trophies, softball trophies, bowling trophies and he even had a badminton trophy and a horseshoes trophy. My brother, in his younger years, inherited many of my father's athletic genes. Unfortunately, they skipped past me for a few years. I used to look at my dad's trophy case in awe, wondering if I would ever have any to add to the collection.

My dad had hopes that I would tap into some athleticism in my 3rd grade year so he signed me up for Little League. I'm embarrassed to admit it, but I was not a good baseball player. My main problem was that I was afraid of being hit by the ball. So, every time the ball was pitched to me I'd either jump out of the batter's box or stand there and watch the ball go across the plate without ever swinging the bat. The only way I ever got on base was either by being walked or being hit by the pitcher. So, there I was, the son of a renowned athlete, bringing dishonor to the family name. I went through an entire season without ever swinging the bat.

As I recall, it was the last game of the season. My dad had been telling me for weeks, "You can do it. You can hit the ball. But first you've got to swing the bat!" I guess what he said finally registered with me. The final game I was determined that I was going to swing the bat, even if I struck out. I mean, really, striking out while swinging the bat is at least more impressive than striking out standing there. So I did it, I swung the bat. To my complete surprise I actually connected with the ball and it went sailing into centerfield. I was shocked! I started running... and kept on running. I made it to third base! My first time to actually swing the bat got me a triple!

I didn't win a trophy that year. I got something much more important. I felt my father's pride in me... not because I got a triple, but because I overcame my fear and swung the bat. I trusted what he said, and then I did what he said, and the results followed.

Child of God, we are sons and daughters of a victorious Father. He has never been defeated. His trophy case is full from all His victories. He's been telling you, "You can do it! You can succeed! Just do what I told you." So, lay aside your fears, and all your excuses... and SWING THE BAT!

INDEX

Made in the USA
Las Vegas, NV
17 March 2024

87338900R00108